THE BICYCLING WINE TOURIST

Hidden Gems in Oregon Wine Country

CLAUDIA HARRINGTON

Contents

Dedication

Dedicated to all the passionate vintners who take no shortcuts in creating a superior wine and to the tasting room associates who showcase it.

Intro

This book started as a strategy to get me back on my bicycle. Riding was something I loved to do but had neglected as other priorities steadily encroached. A longtime Portland native, I had finished my winemaking and viticulture management classes at Chemeketa Community College in Salem, Oregon. Winemaking constituted an encore career I had always dreamed of, but one I would have to pursue while still keeping my day job.

I was working in a tasting room, making little more than minimum wage, while still working 24 hours a week as a special care nurse for critical newborns. Holding down two jobs is not unusual in the wine industry, but it left me with little time outside of work to do the things I wanted to do. On days off there was a never-ending slew of home and yard maintenance projects.

Thinking that over, I realized that in my time off, I was only accomplishing activities that had deadlines: weed and mulch the flower garden today, transplant those petunias this weekend, on top of regularly scheduled activities like making meals, washing dishes, and cleaning house. Each job had a deadline, and it got done. Maybe I could make riding my bike into something with a fixed deadline? Knowing my propensity for procrastination, and my already busy schedule, it just wasn't going to happen otherwise.

Out of that realization, this project was born. I would put together a series of fun rides to wineries in Oregon and Washington. And as for the deadline? The end of summer 2013 sounded feasible. I could share the rides with friends, and I envisioned typing them up into a little booklet that would be handy to take along on rides.

Little did I know this project would take on a life of its own, and two years later I would finally be putting the finishing touches on my book.

Which wineries to choose? Oregon has over 400 wineries alone. The wineries I decided to explore were those using grapes that were grown organically and biodynamically. In the wine world these are still the most unusual. Could one taste the difference? Perhaps this would be a fun question to explore.

How many rides would I map out? Ten seemed like a nice round number, and I visualized myself driving down to southern Oregon to complete a ride or two each weekend during the summer.

How many wineries to include in each ride? Any more than three wineries in a day, and I have found my palate dulls beyond the point of being able to differentiate the subtleties between wines. The rides in this book, therefore, include between two and three wineries apiece.

Since I prefer my bicycle rides to be a loop, I have included that option even though it may include gravel roads. There is usually also an out-and-back option to keep you on a paved road.

As I was doing research for this book, it became clear that sustainable viticulture forms the backbone of both organic and biodynamic viticulture practices. The wineries I have chosen to include in these rides all feature grapes that are grown sustainably (more about this later), and all ten rides take place in the Upper Willamette Valley or the Columbia River Gorge.

After I had mapped out all ten rides, I realized I needed to provide guidance on where to take a break, where to eat, where to stay, where to rent bikes, how to send wines home, and more. Not only that, each area has special features I felt were not to be missed – like that delectable artisan cheese maker outside Salem, and some of the quirks of little towns, such as the logic used in naming Dallas. I've tried to provide this guidance as much as possible throughout this book, but I also hope readers will explore for themselves and make new discoveries along the way.

Vintage Wine Making Equipment

A little bit about Oregon wine

In less than 50 years Oregon has grown from a handful of wineries to over 400. The flagship grape is Pinot Noir, and it has yearly collected accolades. 2012's November Wine Spectator names Oregon the New World home of Pinot Noir, the "Old World" of course being Burgundy, France.

Some say the uniqueness of the wine stems from the geology that has formed the Oregon soils. During the last ice age, the Missoula Floods cascaded through the Gorge and into the Willamette Valley, depositing varying amounts of soils vastly different from one another in close proximity. (See further discussion of soil importance and AVAs in **Definitions).**

Some say it's about *terroir,* the French word that is all-encompassing of the natural environment in which a wine is produced. Terroir is about climate, temperature, soil, aspect, and altitude affecting the resulting grapes

Some say it's the care each vine receives. You will find very few large "corporate" vineyards or wineries in Oregon. Most are boutique, family-owned vineyards, whose owners lavish meticulous care on their vines, creating limited vintages of exquisite quality and unique properties.

The bike rides you'll find in this book will take you to 24 such wineries, frequently along routes less-traveled. In many cases, the proprietors of the wineries are also the owners. Ask them what sustainable vineyard care means to them, and why it matters for all of us who care about good wine and the places where the grapes grow.

How to use this book

Each ride has:

1. A summary of the ride, a brief description of the towns at your starting point, and turn by turn direction of that ride.

2. A map of the ride, followed by tables containing running totals of mileage and mileage from one point to the next. The white squared numbers on the map indicate the mileage markers for the ride. The green circled numbers correspond to the suggested directions.

   The turn-by-turn directions have the most detail. The maps give a general location with some roads marked but may lack detail. The mileage tables which are designed to be folded in 4ths, contain running totals of mileage (first column) and mileage from point to point, (second column). The white squared numbers indicate the mileage markers for the ride. The green circled numbers correspond to the suggested directions. The letters indicate the location of the winery reviewed. I carried both the map and tables in my front pack for quick references. Snap a photo with your phone and enlarge as needed.

3. The letters indicate the location of a winery reviewed.

What to expect?

Because most wineries sit atop a hill, these rides will require that you have some bicycling experience and have at least begun working on your "climbing legs." A road bike is probably your best choice for most of the rides, however some rides do traverse a fair amount of gravel (maps are marked), and these rides will be more enjoyable if you have a bike that doesn't balk at the loose stuff.

No records need to be set. You can take your time, stop and rest, and soak in the scenery. Oregon wine country tends toward green rolling hills, dotted with farms, grazing sheep and even llamas! On a clear day, you may see on the horizon Mount Hood, Mount Adams, and Mount Saint Helens, which last erupted in 1980, losing its perfect peak. Small wineries are wonderful places to relax and focus on the nuances of wine, and many have spectacular views from their tasting rooms.

Note: Always call the wineries before your visit, as their hours may have changed or they may be closed for special events.

Supplies

Don't forget your bicycle helmet and riding gloves. Plenty of water and satisfying snacks are also a must. The days can be warm, so plan accordingly in your bicycle wear. Dressing in layers is usually best. Make sure your bike is in good working order and carry enough equipment to at least change a tire, should the need arise.

Moderation is key when it comes to tasting and riding. If you feel you need to wait to begin riding again, do. Please don't think of this as a "winery-crawl." This is about finding that perfect wine that simply must come home with you.

Definitions

American Viticultural Areas (AVAs)

AVAs have been designated both by physical boundaries and by the types of soils found within those boundaries. In Oregon there are presently 11 AVAS and four AVAs that are shared with another state. Many people believe that you can taste the difference in wine grown in each AVA. Real Estate has become very expensive in coveted AVAs.

The bike rides in this book will take you to eight Oregon AVAs and one that is shared with Washington State.

Certification and its meanings

The wineries included in these rides are, for the most part, Certified Sustainable, Organic, or Demeter Certified Biodynamic.

Here's why that matters and what it means.

An impressive number of Oregon's vineyards are certified sustainable. Fewer are organic, and even fewer are biodynamic. And, for many of those who don't yet have certification, sustainability is still both a priority and a lifestyle. The benefits are two-fold:

1. Research indicates (and there is ample local evidence) that roots of organically farmed grapes are less vulnerable than those of conventionally grown vines to pathogens such as the Phylloxera root louse. (Lotter, Granett, & Omer. HortScience 34(6): 1108-1111. 1999).
2. Farm runoff accounts for up to 60% of pollutants and all the associated ills to surrounding watersheds and fish. (USGS. Annotated Bibliography-Tualatin River Basin studies. Updated

6/20/2012).

Organic Certification

Wineries in Oregon obtain certification through **TILTH**, a nonprofit research and education membership organization dedicated to biologically sound and socially equitable agriculture. This is a yearly process. The focus is pesticides and fertilizers, as well as additives used in winemaking. In addition, barrier rules apply separating organic fields from non-organic. **TILTH** in Oregon has been offering certification services since the early 1980's. (www.TILTH.org).

Sustainability Certification

In Oregon sustainability certification is obtained through LIVE (**Low Input Viticulture and Enology**), and must be renewed yearly. A broader certification than **TILTH,** LIVE includes the care of the land as well as the employees. It has partnered with two other related organizations, Salmon Safe and OCSW (Oregon Certified Sustainable Wine). LIVE also administers the **Carbon Reduction Challenge (CRC)**, a certification aimed at helping wineries achieve energy efficiencies and addressing greenhouse gas emissions in the Pacific Northwest wine industry. For many vineyards, the Sustainability Certification forms the backbone of the organic vineyard. LIVE has been certifying growers in Oregon since 1999 and in Washington since 2006. It has recently expanded its geographical boundaries to include all of the Pacific Northwest, including British Columbia and Idaho (www.LIVEinc.org).

There are six objectives that must be met:
1. To see the vineyard as a whole system.
2. To create and maintain viticulture that is economically viable over time.
3. To maintain the highest level of quality in fruit production. Production shouldn't require compromise of quality standards.

4. To implement cultural practices and solve problems that minimize the use of agricultural chemicals and fertilizers, with the goal of protecting the farmer, environment, and society at large.
5. To encourage farming practices promoting and maintaining high biological diversity in the whole vineyard.
6. To encourage responsible stewardship of soil health, fertility, and stability .

According to LIVE's website, there are currently 204 vineyards and 26 wineries with Certification status. (www.LIVEinc.org).

Biodynamic Certification
This certification is obtained through the Demeter Association, Inc., the U.S. representative of Demeter International. This is a nonprofit organization, incorporated in 1985, whose mission is to enable people to farm successfully, in accordance with Biodynamic practices and principles. Demeter's vision of Biodynamics has much in common with other organic approaches: To heal the planet through agriculture (www.demeterbta.com).

This method credits Rudolf Steiner, an anthroposopher and somewhat of an enigma, as its founder. The international certification for **Demeter Biodynamics** began in 1928. The method employs manures, herbs, and compost prepared in a very specific way. It prohibits the use of all artificial chemicals. Methods unique to the biodynamic approach include an emphasis on integrating farm animals into the farming system, the use of fermented herbal and mineral preparations as compost additive and field sprays, and the use of an astrological sowing and planting calendar.

Biodynamic practices are somewhat controversial. Some critics compare it to a religion. The preparations, generally called "preps," require multiple steps, which must be done in a defined step-wise (some would say rigid) manner. Biodynamic farming is probably best known for its incorporation of manure into cow horns, which are then buried in autumn at a prescribed depth and dug up the following spring to be added to the compost pile. Actually lots of animal parts are needed as containers for various preparations, and herbs such as chamomile, nettles, and valerian are essential parts of the process. Many of these preps are sprayed directly on the vines, rather than used as top-dressing for the soil.

Many of the vineyards that incorporate this method are small. The resulting wine *can* be extraordinary, but very labor-intensive. Some of the larger vineyards using the method rely on expensive consultants, expensive custom machinery, and commercial preparations of each of the preps.

So, the cost of this approach can be minimal (but labor-intensive) or very expensive…some say more expensive then farming conventionally.

An excellent resource if you would like to learn more about biodynamic farming in Oregon is **Voodoo Vintners, Oregon's Astonishing Biodynamic Winegrowers,** by Katherine Cole.

Perhaps one of the best examples of the biodynamic method is Montinore Estate, located just outside of Forest Grove, Oregon. Owned by Rudy Marchesi, Montinore Estate produces excellent wines at affordable prices. As detailed by Cole, this vineyard has a farm mechanic, Don Huggett, who has a gift for inventing whatever contraption they need. All of the special equipment to stir, pulverize, spread and spray preparations or mow weeds he has "rigged-up" from various parts of cars, pick-ups, farm machinery, etc.

What's more, sheep are trucked in by a local rancher to munch weeds.

The resulting grapes arrive in the winery uniformly ripe with desirable characteristics that play out in the wine. Winemaker John Lundy calls the approach "just letting the farm show through."

Montinore Estate is achieving the ultimate – wines biodynamically farmed and made "naturally" in the winery (similar to many European wines) for a fraction of the cost of many similarly made wines.

Ultimately, is there a difference?

Many winemakers believe that the results of the viticultural methods described above result in brighter, more flavorful wine that better reflect the characteristics of the land from which they are grown.

What do I think?

I have tasted some marvelous wines and also some with flaws. I suspect that regardless of how the grape was grown, the winemaker has the ultimate influence, as the wine is carefully guided through each step of winemaking to its final outcome.

You'll need to taste for yourself to see if you agree.

photo opposite page:

Cow horn manure, one of the hallmarks of biodynamics.

Photo credit: Andie Long

1 Forest Grove Loop

This ride starts from Rogers Park and avoids (for the most part) busy roads. It includes Montinore Estate and Patton Valley Vineyards. Think of it as a "figure eight." You will ride a section of Spring Hill Rd both coming and going. Of course you could ride it differently (see map). It meanders along rolling hills through farmland, but the only real hill is the driveway to Patton Valley Vineyard.
Total distance: 19 miles.

Forest Grove, population 21,000, is about 25 miles west of Portland and considered a bedroom suburb. It is home to Pacific University and has a charming and thriving downtown.

Where to eat. You might want to get a sandwich at **1910 Main** on 19th Avenue and Main Street in Forest Grove, or just wait until you reach Gaston and go to the not-to-be-missed **Pretty Good Grocery** (aka Gaston Market). Elena, one of owners, is happy to make you a sandwich from a fresh baguette with your choice of filling, including vegetarian options. She'll offer you tastes of the cheeses she has available (a wide range of European and local cheese). She'll also entice you with lots of other fresh accoutrements and let you refill your water bottles. Or, if you're ready for a sit-down-inside stop, you might consider Gaston's **One Horse Tavern,** one block south, for a juicy hamburger.

Head west on 17th Ave.
Turn L onto B St.
1.9 mi **Take 2nd R** onto SW Old Hwy 47.

2.4 mi **Turn R** onto SW Hiatt Rd.

2.6 mi **Turn L** onto SW Dilly.

Montinore Estate is on the left through the large wrought-iron gates and up the winding paved driveway.

Turn R on SW Dilley when you leave the winery.2.9 mi **Turn L** onto SW Dudney Ave.

3.0 mi **Turn R** onto Hwy 47 S / Tualatin Valley Hwy (a busy road but it has a nice wide shoulder).

3.7 mi **Turn L** onto SW Spring Hill Rd.

mi **Turn R** onto SW Gaston Rd, which turns into Main. (The park on L next to the Fire Station makes a good rest stop).

mi **Turn R** onto Front St (Tualatin Valley Hwy). Look for Old Oregon 47 N on left.

8 mi **Turn L** and follow Old Oregon 47 N. It does some meandering.

9.8 mi **Patton Valley Vineyards** is on **L**. The sign is also on the left. The tasting room is up a 0.7 mi curving gravel road. The tasting room manager Danielle Ball says there's free tasting to cyclists who make it up the driveway.

When you leave Patton Valley Vineyards, **Turn L**. to continue on Old Oregon 47.

10.9 mi **Turn R**. onto SW Spring Hill. Rd 11.6 mi **Turn L** onto Fern Hill Rd. 15.6 mi the road becomes Maple Street.

Turn L onto 18th Ave and another **L**. on Elm, and turn **R**. onto 17th which brings you back to Rogers Park.

Montinore Estate
(Biodynamic, Demeter Certified)

N. Willamette Valley AVA
3663 Dilley Rd,
Forest Grove, OR 97116
503-359-5012
www.montinore.com

Hours: 11 a.m. - 5 p.m. daily (closed major holidays)
Tasting Fee: $5 for flight of 5
Production: 36,000 cases/year
Owner: Rudy Marchesi

Winemakers: Ben Thomas is in charge of red wine (Pinot Noir), and Stephen Webber covers the whites.

About: The vines were planted in 1982, and production began in 1987. The vineyard has been Demeter Certified Biodynamic since 2008.

Wines
   Whites: Pinot Gris, Gewürztraminer, Rieslings and dessert wines.
   Reds: Pinots from four different blocks, plus a Rosé.

Tasting Notes

There are many choices and something to please everyone, with styles ranging from dry to sweet dessert wines.

I loved the crisp, flowery taste of the dry Gewürztraminer

The price-point overall is very reasonable. Even the estate blend of Pinot Noir is just $20

Patton Valley Vineyard (Certified LIVE)
N. Willamette Valley AVA
9449 SW Old Hwy 47, Gaston
OR 97119
503-985-3445
www.pattonvalley.com

Hours: 11 a.m. – 5 p.m. Thursday – Monday
Tasting Fee: $10, refundable with $30 purchase
Production: 3,500 – 4,000 cases/year
Owner: Monte Pitt
Winemaker: Derek Einberger
About: The first vintage was in 1999.

Wines

Depending on the year, there are five Pinots, a Syrah and a Rosé.

Tasting Notes

The wines have structure and depth. The Rosé (Pinot Noir) is seasonal. It was crisp with strawberry notes, the perfect wine for a summer day.

The tasting room is very informal, one big room with cases of wine against the wall and a counter for tasting/buying wine. There are picnic benches outside.

Forest Grove Loop

A. Montinore Estate, 3663 SW Dilley Rd. Forest Grove. OR97116

B. Pretty Good Market,

C. Patton Valley Vineyards, Tualatin Valley Hwy, Gaston, OR 97119

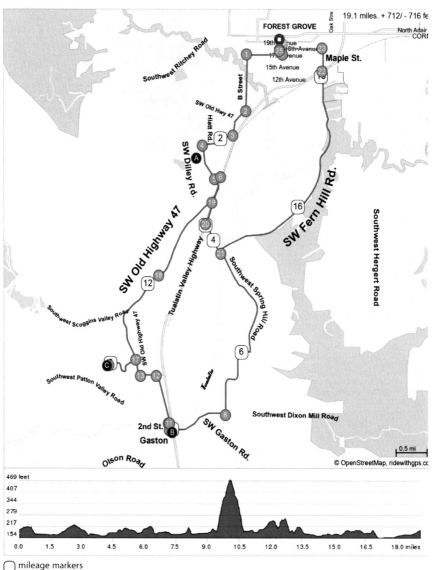

mileage markers

suggested directions

20

Forest Grove Loop

0.0	0.0	☐	Start of route
0.6	0.6	←	head west on 17th from the park. L onto B St
1.4	0.8	→	R onto SW Old Hwy 47
1.8	0.4	→	R onto SW Hiatt Rd
2.3	0.5	←	L onto SW Dilley Rd. Watch for entrace to Montinore Estates. The driveway is paved.
2.9	0.5	←	L onto SW Dudney Ave
3.0	0.1	→	R onto OR-47 S/Tualatin Valley Hwy
3.7	0.7	←	L onto SW Spring Hill Rd
7.1	3.4	→	R onto SW Gaston Rd
8.1	1.0	→	R onto 2nd St

8.1 miles. +220/-216 feet

8.2	0.1	→	R onto Mill St
8.2	0.0	←	L onto SW Old Highway 47
8.9	0.7	←	L to stay on SW Old Highway 47
9.2	0.3	→	R to stay on SW Old Highway 47
9.4	0.3	←	L into Patton Valley Vineyards. The curving gravel driveway is .7 mi
10.0	0.6	←	L as you leave back onto Old Hwy 47
10.1	0.1	→	R toward SW Old Highway 47
10.7	0.6	←	L onto SW Old Highway 47
12.2	1.5	→	Slight R to stay on SW Old Highway 47
13.6	1.4	→	R onto OR-47 S/Tualatin Valley Hwy

5.6 miles. +485/-495 feet

14.0	0.3	←	L onto SW Spring Hill Rd
14.5	0.5	←	L onto SW Fern Hill Rd
18.1	3.6	↑	Continue onto Maple St
18.4	0.3	←	L onto 18th Ave
19.1	0.7	←	L onto Douglas St and back to Rogers Park, your start/finish point
19.1	0.0	☐	End of route

5.5 miles. +124/-101 feet

2 NEWBERG LOOP

*This ride begins at the intersection of Old Portland Road (99 W) and Springbrook Road and goes up into the Chehalem Mountains AVA. It includes three wineries: Adelsheim, Bergstrom, and J. Christopher (NOTE: J. Christopher requires advance notice for tasting). This ride does lots of climbing. **Two** options are offered. One of the options is an "out-and-back," which offers rolling hills with some climbing. For those who need their ride to be a loop, there are about six miles (intermittent) of gravel, quite a bit of it uphill. Even this route has an option which includes a downhill run on Bald Peak Road that has beautiful pavement and gorgeous views of the valley.*

Newberg, population about 22,000, is a fairly large town by Willamette Valley standards. It's located about 25 miles southwest of Portland and is home to George Fox University. Of historical note, from 1885-1891 President Herbert Hoover lived here with his aunt and uncle (John and Laura Minthorn), who were administrators of what was to become George Fox University. The house, now a museum, is located at 115 S. River St.

Newberg's main drag is Highway 99 (Old Portland Road). You'll find every imaginable fast food franchise along here. There are also large grocery stores, and many other businesses. The downtown area is quite small and authentically quaint. More and more tasting rooms are popping up in this little area.

Where to eat.

If you're in a hurry for a quick pick-me-up, you might try the **Coffee**

Cottage (808 E. Hancock St). They have a drive-up window and are open 6am-10pm. More importantly they have a daily variety of fresh-baked scones. If, instead, you're thinking along the lines of a sandwich, Newburg's franchises are along Highway 99. Most of the large grocery stores have delis that will make sandwiches to go. Maybe you're looking for something a little special? Try **Recipe (115 N. Washington St.).** This restaurant is open for lunch at 11:30 a.m. and will cheerfully make your order "take out." However, you might opt to make Recipe where you go in the evening *after* your ride. They have fresh, in-season, locally sourced food and an extensive local wine selection.

If you want more variety and have a little time, continue on Highway 99 to Dundee just a few more miles and try **The Red Hills Market (155 SW 7ᵗʰ St, Dundee**). They're open daily 7a.m.– 8p.m. and have a blackboard full of various sandwiches, wood-fired pizzas, and beverage choices.

To begin this ride, look for the large shopping center on the NE corner of the intersection of Old Portland Rd. and Springbrook Rd. This works well for parking. **Turn R** as you leave the parking area and head N. up Springbrook Rd. At the traffic circle, continue straight to stay on N. Springbrook Rd.

0.9 mi After slight curve, road becomes Mountainview Dr. **Turn R** onto NE Zimri Dr. and head up a hill
1.9 mi **Turn L** onto Bell Rd.
2.9 mi When Bell crosses College St (NE Hillsboro Hwy, Bald Peak Rd) it becomes North Valley Rd.
6.9 mi **Turn R** onto Calkins Rd. and begin climbing.

7.4 mi Watch for the entrance to **Adelsheim winery** on the right. On leaving turn **Right** and continue up Calkins.

8.0 mi Watch for **Bergstrom winery** on the left. Driveway is short but uphill. On leaving **Turn L** and continue a little more uphill where the road begins to level out and become a little country road that winds past farmyards.

(Option 1: The out-and-back version)

9.6 mi **Turn L** on Dopp Rd. and head downhill to North Valley and retrace your path. **Turn L** on NE Hillside Dr and climb 0.5 miles on gravel over old asphalt to **J. Christopher winery** on the right. On leaving, **Turn L** and head back down the hill. **Turn L** on North Valley Rd. and retrace path to the shopping center in Newberg.

(Option 2: Loop)

9.6 mi **Turn R** on Dopp Rd. Road becomes gravel right after you pass the big red barn on the right.
11.2 mi **Turn R** onto NE Tykeson (still gravel) and begin climbing.
12.6 mi **Turn L** onto NE Kings Grade (gravel, more climbing…).
13.1 mi **Turn R** onto SW Finnigan Hill Rd, (gravel, still climbing). This is a "short-cut" to Bald Peak Rd.
13.2 mi **Turn R** onto SW Bald Peak Rd. and head downhill. Beautiful pavement, beautiful views!
16.0 mi **Turn R** onto NE Chehalem and watch for Hillside Dr (it's easy to miss).
16.3 mi **Turn R** onto NE Hillside Dr. This road quickly becomes gravel, but not too bad.

18.0 mi Watch for **J. Christopher winery** on the left. On leaving, continue downhill to North Valley Rd.

18.5 mi **Turn L** back onto NE North Valley and start back to town.

21.1 mi Cross Hillsboro Hwy/College and road becomes Bell Rd.

21.4 mi **Turn R** onto N. Aspen Way.

22.7 mi **Turn L**. onto Mountainview Dr.

23.0 mi Continue straight onto N. Springbrook Rd.

23.2 mi At the traffic circle, continue straight to stay on Springbrook Rd.

24.0 mi Return to Shopping Center, your start/finish point.

Adelsheim
(Sustainable, LIVE Certified)
Chehalem Mountains AVA
16800 NE Calkins Lane, Newberg, OR 97132
503-538-3652
www.adelsheim.com

Hours: 11 a.m. – 4 p.m. daily

Tasting fee $15, waived for purchase of any wine on daily "flight" or a minimum of $45 on available wines.

Production: 45,000 cases/year

Owner: David Adelsheim

Winemaker: Dave Paige

About: 1978 was the first vintage year. This winery can be classified as one of the pioneers of the Willamette Valley. It's still family-run.

Wines

The daily flight usually is composed of Pinot Noir from various vineyards (most owned by Adelsheim), and at least one Chardonnay.

There are other choices such as Pinot Gris, Pinot Blanc, and the unusual Auxerrois, which may not be available for tasting, but definitely ask about it!

<u>Tasting Notes</u>

The various Pinots were delightful but the wine that held our attention most was the Auxerrois. This white wine, whose original home is in the Alsace, France, is rare in the Willamette Valley. A dry wine, it has the floral notes of a Pinot Blanc.

Bergstrom (Biodynamic, Demeter Certifed)
Chehalem Mountains AVA
18215 NE Calkins Lane, Newberg,97132
503-554-0468
www.bergstromwine.com

Hours: daily 11-4
Tasting Fee, $15, waived with purchase of $100.
Owner: Jointly owned by John and Karen Bergstrom and Josh and Caroline Bergstrom.
Wine maker: Josh Bergstrom
Yearly Production about 13,000 cases/yearly

History: 1999 was the first release. Currently encompasses 5 estate vineyards that span 4 of the Willamette Valley's appellations. This winery is still very much family-run.

<u>Tasting notes:</u>

With four different AVAs represented you can really have a sense of how terroir affects the pinot noirs represented.

There are 2 chardonnays.

Of the wines we had, I found the 2011 Old Stones Chardonnay to be unique. It had been barreled and left on "the lees" (spent yeast hulls) for a year before bottling. It had lots of complexity, nuttiness and citrus notes.

J. Christopher Vineyard, (Biodynamic Principles) Chehalem AVA 17150 NE Hillside Dr. Newberg, Or. 97132 503-554-9572
www.jchristopherwines.com

Hours: 7 days a week, 11-4pm (by appointment)
Tasting fee: $10, waived with $200 purchase
Owners: Jay Somers and Ernst Loosen
Winemaker: Jay Somers
Production: about 5,000 cases/year

History: Jay Somers made his first commercial wine in 1996. He has always had a passion for Burgundian style pinot noir. He worked in a variety of places not only here in the valley but in New Zealand, and Germany. It was during a harvest in Germany that he and Ernst Loosen (owner and winemaker of Dr. Loosen Winery) developed a long-term friendship and a plan for launching a vineyard and a winery in Oregon to develop Oregonian pinot that showcases old world style . The 40 acre vineyard is still young and Somers is sourcing fruit from vineyards in four different AVAs, (Chehalem Mountains, Dundee Hills, Eola-Amity Hills, and Yamhill-Carlton)

<u>Wines:</u>

Sauvignon Blanc, Chardonnay, four different Pinot Noirs

<u>Tasting Notes:</u>

All of the wines were note-worthy but I especially liked the Sauvignon Blanc. To me it was very much like the Sauvignon Blancs from the Loire Valley; crisp and clear, aromatic, with notes of green apples and flowers with enough tartness to give it freshness.

The '07 Appassionata Pinot Noir lived up to its reputation with lots of complexity; dark fruit, some earthiness, tannins to give it structure, and a wonderful silky mouth-feel.

Newberg Loop

A. Adelsheim winery

C. J Christopher winery

B. Bergstrom winery

Newberg Loop

0.0	0.0	☐	Start of route
0.6	0.6	↑	Leave shopping center parking and R onto Springbrook Rd.At the traffic circle, continue straight to stay on N Springbrook Rd
0.9	0.2	↑	Continue onto E Mountainview Dr
0.9	0.1	→	R onto NE Zimri Dr
1.9	0.9	←	L onto NE Bell Rd
2.9	1.0	↑	Continue onto NE North Valley Rd

2.9 miles. +329/-172 feet

6.9	4.1	→	R onto NE Calkins Ln. Watch for Adelsheim entrace on R On leaving R and continue up hill. Bergstrom entrance will be on L On leaving L and continue on Calkins Ln
8.9	2.0	←	L to stay on NE Calkins Ln
9.6	0.8	→	R onto NE Dopp Rd. Road quickly become gravel
11.2	1.6	→	R onto NE Tykeson Rd and begin climbing, still on gravel
12.6	1.4	←	L onto NE Kings Grade, more gravel, still climbing

9.7 miles. +858/-226 feet

13.1	0.6	→	R onto SW Finnigan Hill Rd, gravel. This will take you through to Bald Peak
13.2	0.1	→	Slight R onto SW Bald Peak Rd, beautiful pavement, beautiful views of the valley. (Option: Skip J. Christopher and take this road to Bell Road to return back to starting point
16.0	2.8	→	R onto NE Chehalem Dr
16.3	0.2	→	R onto NE Hillside Dr. Quickly becomes gravel but not bad
16.6	0.3	←	L to stay on NE Hillside Dr. Watch for J. Christopher driveway on L

4.0 miles. +168/-668 feet

17.9	1.4	←	L to stay on NE Hillside Dr
18.5	0.5	←	L back onto NE North Valley Rd
21.1	2.6	↑	Continue onto NE Bell Rd
21.4	0.3	→	R onto N Aspen Way
22.7	1.3	←	L onto E Mountainview Dr
23.0	0.2	↑	Continue straight onto N Springbrook Rd
23.2	0.2	↑	At the traffic circle, continue straight to stay on N Springbrook Rd. in at shopping center parking lot, your start/finish point
23.4	0.2	☐	End of route

6.9 miles. +370/-422 feet

3 YAMHILL LOOP

This ride has some wonderful country roads, and some steep hills. It includes WillaKenzie Estate, Trisaetum, and Penner-Ash Wineries. There are quite a few excellent wineries along this route that you may want to visit, as well. Therefore, this ride may be worth repeating in order to include them all. Beaux Frere and Brick House, in particular, are outstanding, though they require advance appointment for tastings. Total distance is about 26 miles.

Yamhill, population 1,000, is a charming little town that still has many of its original buildings. Its business area is pretty much one street (Main Street). Its general store, established 1903, will sell you groceries, make you a sandwich, sell you a "double-bitted" ax... or a vintage dresser! The annual Derby Days publishes a newsletter that includes lots of the town's firsts. The 2012 Derby Days newsletter, for example, informed people that "Yamhill was the first of small towns in Oregon to have electric lights in 1902. It also boasted rural telephones and a concrete paved street in 1906."

Where to eat.

Sandwiches can be had from the general store. Zippy's might be your choice for pizza, hamburger/fries and a frosty beer/ale.

You might consider Beulah Park for your lunch stop or just a rest stop after your ride.

In Yamhill, parking is generally plentiful. If school isn't in session, the parking lot of the Yamhill/Carlton Intermediate school is a good option.

Leaving the school, **Turn L** and head south on Hwy 240.

1.5 mi **Turn L** at Laughlin Rd.

2.5 mi **Turn L** into **WillaKenzie Estate.**

Turn L as you leave WillaKenzie to continue on Laughlin Rd.

5.7 mi **Turn R** onto North Valley Rd.

You will pass **Beaux Frere Vineyards** on the left. You will see signage for **Trisaetum**, but resist following…it's all uphill gravel! Here's a better option:

9.6 mi **Turn L** Follow North Valley when it makes a dog-leg.

10.3 mi **Turn L** onto Lewis Rogers Lane. *(11.7 mi **Brick House** is on the right).*

11.8 mi **Turn R** on Ribbon Ridge Rd. You can see **Trisaetum's** large, wrought-iron gates from here.

11.9 mi **Trisaetum Winery** is on the left.

On leaving, retrace path to North Valley Rd via Lewis Rogers and **Turn R** onto North Valley Rd.

14.2 mi **Turn L** onto Ribbon Ridge Rd.

14.5 mi **Penner-Ash Winery** is on the right, up a long curving mostly-paved driveway.

On leaving, **Turn L** back onto Ribbon Ridge Rd and go up to the intersection and stay to the left, which will be North Valley Rd.

20.2 mi **Turn L** onto Flett Rd.

21.6 mi **Turn L** onto Hwy 47. Arrive in Yamhill on Maple Ave

27.3 mi **Turn L** (blinking yellow) onto Main St. The school will be on your left.

WillaKenzie Estate
(Sustainable, LIVE Certified)
Yamhill Carlton AVA
19143 NE Laughlin Rd, Yamhill, OR
97148 503-662-3280
www.willakenzie.com

Hours: daily 10 a.m.–4 p.m. (Nov.-Apr.) / 10 a.m.–5 p.m. (May-Oct.)
Tasting Fee $20, waived with $60 purchase.
Production: 20,000 cases/year
Owner: Bernard Lacroute
Winemaker: Thibaud Mandet

About: The winery was a long-time dream for owner, Bernard Lacroute. Both from France, the owner and winemaker of this twenty-two year old winery shared the goal of producing wine in the Old World style with the best of American innovations.

Wines

Wines in the tasting room vary by month. They may include Pinot Gris, Pinot Blanc, Chardonnay, and various Pinot Noirs.

Tasting Notes

The 2011 Pinot Blanc was especially delightful. It was lemony, and crisp with a long finish

A favored Pinot Noir was the 2009 Terres Basses, a structured wine with plenty of tannin and classic Pinot Noir nuances of dark fruit, cedar, tobacco, with a silky mouth-feel.

Trisaetum Winery
(Sustainable, LIVE Certified)
Ribbon Ridge AVA
18401 NE Ribbon Ridge Rd, Newberg, OR 97132
503-538-9898
www.trisaetum.com

Hours: 11 a.m. - 4 p.m. Wednesday - Monday
Tasting Fee: $10, waived with purchase of one bottle
Production: 6,000 cases/year
Owner/ Winemaker: James Frey

About: The name, Trisaetum, is the combination of names of the owner's son, Tristen, and his daughter, Tatum.

2007 was Trisaetum's first commercial vintage. What sets this winery apart from its peers is the art gallery, featuring paintings and photography by James Frey, as well as the 100 foot long barrel cave, where finished wine is cellared.

Tasting Notes

The winery produces wine from its own three vineyards, which total 58 acres. These wines, all different styles, are derived from Pinot Noir and Reisling. A wine that I found unique was a Pinot Noir called Nuit Blanche (white Pinot Noir). Fermented like a red wine, it aged for a year in oak barrels. Its mouth-feel is creamy with lots of floral notes.

Penner-Ash Wine Cellars
(Sustainable, Live Certified)
Yamhill-Carlton AVA
15771 NE Ribbon Ridge Road, Newberg, OR 97132
503-554 5545
www.pennerash.com

Hours: 11 a.m. – 5 p.m. daily
Tasting Fee: daily flight $15, waived for $90 purchase
Production: 9,000 cases/year
Owners: Ron and Lynn Penner-Ash
Winemaker: Lynn Penner-Ash

About: Lynn has been actively involved in the wine industry since 1988. After years working for other wineries, Ron and Lynn built Penner-Ash. Their first vintage was in 1998.

Wines

White: Viognier, Riesling, Roseo (Rosé)
Red: Three Pinot Noirs, Rubeo (Pinot/Syrah blend), Syrah

Tasting Notes

The Viognier was my favorite. It had good balance and perhaps the best descriptor is the one they use: lemon custard.

The Pinots were all winners. Bella Vida Pinot Noir was incredibly smooth with flavors of rose petals and hints of tobacco.

The Bicycling Wine Tourist

Yamhill Loop

A. WillaKensie Estate, Northwest Adcock Rd. Rd. Yamhill, OR. 97148

B. Trisaetum Winery, 18401 Ribbon Ridge Rd, Newberg, OR. 97132

C. Penner-Ash Cellars, 157 NE Ribbon Ridge Rd. Newberg, OR. 97132

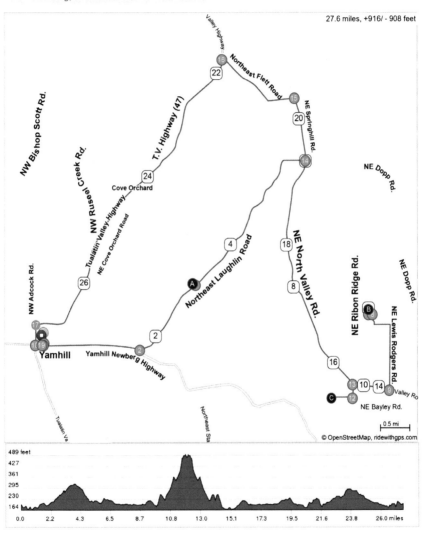

Yamhill Loop

0.0	0.0	☐	Start of route
0.0	0.0	←	L onto E Main St from Yamhill-Carlton Intermediate School
1.6	1.6	←	L onto NE Laughlin Rd
3.0	1.4	←	L into driveway to Willa Kensie Estates
3.2	0.1	←	L onto NE Laughlin Rd
6.0	2.8	→	R onto NE North Valley Rd
10.4	4.4	←	L onto NE Lewis Rogers Ln
12.1	1.7	←	L onto NE Lewis Rogers Ln
12.2	0.1	→	R to stay on Ribbon Ridge Rd. L into Trisaetum Winery

12.2 miles. +677/-379 feet

13.6	1.4	→	Retrace path down to North Valley Rd. R onto NE North Valley Rd
14.5	0.9	←	L onto NE Ribbon Ridge Rd
14.7	0.2	→	R into driveway for Penner-Ash Cellars
15.4	0.7	←	L back onto NE Ribbon Ridge Rd
15.5	0.2	←	Slight L onto NE North Valley Rd
19.4	3.8	↑	Continue onto NE Spring Hill Rd
20.3	1.0	←	L onto NE Flett Rd
21.8	1.4	←	L onto OR-47 S/Tualatin Valley Hwy
27.2	5.4	←	L onto N Maple St

15.0 miles. +432/-445 feet

27.5	0.3	←	L onto State Hwy 240 E/E Main St (signs for Chehalem Valley/Newberg) L. into Yamhill-Carlton Intermediate School your start/finish point
27.6	0.1	☐	End of route

0.4 miles. +3/-0 feet

4 CARLTON LOOP

This is a short loop that includes three wineries. Anne Amie and Lemelson you'll find along the route. After you finish the ride, you will walk down to the third, Lachini Tasting Room. The most elevation gain on the ride occurs on the driveway to Anne Amie. Take a breather when you need to and turn around to look out over the western valley. The views are lovely.

A bicycle trail built on the old railway bed is in the works that will run from Carlton to Hagg Lake. For more information see, www.yamhelaswestsidertrail.com

Founded in 1874 Carlton has a population of about 2,000. Not long ago Carlton was a sleepy little farming town, but with the growth of the wine industry, it has become a destination for wine lovers world-wide. Its main street has blossomed with sandwich shops, bistros, tasting rooms, and creative little what-not shops. The center of town has a small park with trees and picnic tables that adds to the overall ambiance. According to the local government website there are over 40 wineries doing business in Carlton. A bicycle trail built on the old railway bed is in the works that will run from Carlton to Hagg Lake.

Where to eat. You can get good sandwiches to-go at **The Horse Radish** or **Carlton Bakery.**

The ride starts at Upper City Park. Park on a side street.

Head east from the park on Main St, which becomes NE HendricksRd.

1.4 miles **Turn R** onto Mineral Springs Rd.

3.94 miles **Turn L** into **Anne Amie winery** driveway and start up. (driveway is 0.6 miles).

5.2 mi **Turn L** back onto Mineral Springs Rd.

7.4 mi **Turn L** across Hwy 99 (NOTE: *There may be lots of traffic, and it can take some time before you get across*).

Enter the town of Lafayette.

7.7 mi **Turn L** onto Bridge St. As you get out of town the road turns into Abby Road.

Abby Road, for the most part, is a quiet country road that passes farms with pastures and wheat fields and has stretches with large trees partially shading the road.

11.7 mi **Turn L** onto NE Hendricks Rd.

13.3 **Turn R** onto Stag Hollow Rd (gravel road) and onto a short driveway to **Lemelson Vineyards**.

14 mi Return to NE Hendricks Rd and **Turn R.**

15.1 mi arrive back at Upper City Park. Directly in front of the park is Kutch Street and at the end of the block is the **Lachini Tasting Room**.

Anne Amie Vineyards (Sustainable Certified LIVE) Yamhill-Carlton and Chehalem AVAs 6580 Mineral Springs Rd., Carlton, OR 503-864-2991

www.anneamie.com

Hours: 11 a.m. – 5 p.m. daily
Tasting Fee: Varies $10-15, waived for purchases of $50 or more.
Production: 13,000-15,000 cases/year
Owner: Robert Pamplin Jr.
Winemaker: Thomas Houseman

About: In 2000 Chateau Benoit was purchased by the present owner and renamed Anne Amie. Under Robert Pamplin, the winery has achieved high standards and the Pinot Noirs have become extraordinary

Wines

The Winery produces fruit from its own vineyards, as well as a few others.

Whites: Pinot Noir Blanc, Pinot Gris, estate dry Riesling.
Reds: The Pinot Noirs are both single vineyard and blended. There's also a Syrah from Southern Oregon.

Tasting Notes

I found the Viognier to be the one I couldn't resist. It has a crisp minerality with green apples and pears mid-palate.

Yes, the Pinots each had their own personality and were wonderful, but perhaps because it was summer when we visited, my other favorite was the Midnight Saigne, a beautiful pink Róse with lots of strawberry flavors.

Lemelson Vineyards
(Organic Certified TILTH)
Chehalem Mountain, Dundee Hills, & Yamhill-Carlton AVAs
12020 NE Stag Hollow Rd, Carlton, OR 97111
503- 852-6619
www.lemelsonvineyards.com

Hours: 11 a.m.–4 p.m. Thursday–Monday
Tasting Fee: $10, waived with $50 purchase
Production: 11,000-12,000 cases/year
Owner: Eric Lemelson
Winemaker: Anthony King

Wines

    Whites: Pinot Gris, dry Riesling, Chardonnay
    Red: Three single vineyard Pinots and a Pinot blend
    (six different vineyards)

We all differed in our favorites. I found the Meyer vineyard Pinot to have those elements that I most enjoy: dark fruit, some rose petal notes and lots of black tea.

The Pinot Gris had spent some time on the "lees" (spent yeast hulls), which to me gave it welcome depth and complexity.

Lachini Tasting Room
(LIVE Certified + Biodynamic & Organic Practices)
Chehalem Mountain AVA
N. Kutch St., Carlton, OR 97111
503-864-4553
www.lachinivineyards.com

Hours: (Beginning February, 2016) hours Friday-Sunday 12-5
Tasting Fee: $15, waived with $100 purchase
Production 5,000 cases/per year Owners: Ron & Marianne
Winemaker: Laurent Montalieu

About: Ron and Marianne came to Oregon to fulfill a dream—to develop world class Pinot Noir. They started from the ground up. Their vineyard is biodynamically farmed and their emphasis is on Old-World crafting with state-of-the-art technique. Their first vintage was 2001.

Wines

    White: Pinot Gris, Rosé (available in summer only)
    Red: Pinot Noir, Cabernet Sauvignon (Red Mountain, WA)

Tasting Notes

The Oregon Pinot Noir was lush and velvety, full of dark fruit with a touch of vanilla, rounded out with a little smoke and a twist of blueberries.

The Rosé was softer (less acidic) than some with vanilla and strawberry flavors.

Carlton Loop

A. Lemelson Winery   12020 NE Stag Hollow
Road, Carlton, OR

C. Anne Amie Winery, 6580 Mineral Springs
Rd. Carlton OR

B. Lachini Tasting Rm. 258 N. Kutch, Carlton
Or

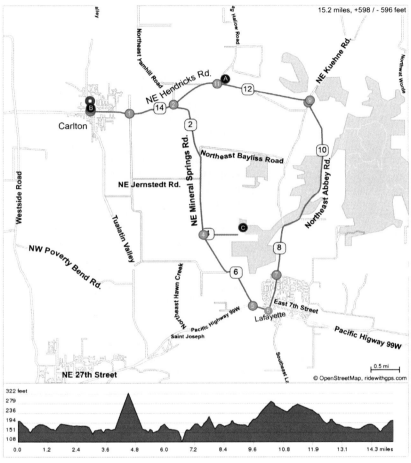

⬭ mileage markers
⬤ suggested directions

45

Carlton Loop

0.0	0.0	▢	Start of route
0.7	0.7	↑	From Upper City Park, Continue onto NE Carlton-Chehalem Creek Rd/NE Hendricks Rd
1.4	0.8	→	R onto NE Mineral Springs Rd
3.9	2.5	←	L up long paved driveway to Anne Amie Winery
5.1	1.2	←	L back onto NE Mineral Springs Rd
6.6	1.6	←	L onto OR-99W N. Very Busy, Take Your Time
6.9	0.3	←	L onto Bridge St
7.6	0.6	↑	Continue onto NE Abbey Rd
10.9	3.3	↑	Continue onto NE Kuehne Rd

10.9 miles. +605/-562 feet

10.9	0.1	←	L onto NE Hendricks Rd.
12.5	1.6	→	R onto NE Stag Hollow Rd, (gravel) follow to Driveway to Lemmelson Winery. R.
12.9	0.4	→	R onto NE Carlton-Chehalem Creek Rd/NE Hendricks Rd. Reenter Carlton on Main St. and return to Upper City Park, start/finish point.
15.2	2.3	→	R onto N Kutch St. Walk to end of block. On R is Lachini Tasting Rm
15.2	0.0	▢	End of route

4.4 miles. +121/-162 feet

5 McMinnville Loop

Over all, this ride is gently rolling hills. The farm roads have little to no shoulder, but at least there is little traffic. This ride includes Eyrie Winery, and Dominio IV (in town), as well as Maysara Winery. It may need a repeat, as there are other wineries along the way that are also worth visiting, including Coeur de Terre, Youngberg Hill, and Coleman Winery. Total distance is about 27 miles.

McMinnville, population 32,000, is about 35 miles southwest of Portland at the confluence of the north and south fork of the Yamhill River. It is home to Linfield College and the Evergreen Aviation Museum.

The thriving downtown has capitalized on its charming old buildings. You'll find kitchen stores, clothing boutiques, book stores, wonderful restaurants and lots of wine tasting rooms in and around the downtown area.

The general plan of the ride is to visit Eyrie, ride out to Maysara, and loop back into town to finish at Dominio IV. But, of course, you can mix it any way you like. There are a couple of cafes at the intersection of Muddy Valley Rd and Hwy 18 if you'd like a stop. I always like to stop at **Farmer John's** (Hwy 18 and Oldsville Rd.), for ice cream and maybe shortcake.

The ride starts from **Eyrie Winery** (935 NE 10th Ave, McMinnville, OR 97128). Parking is plentiful on the side streets in the area.

The best way (by bike) out of town appears to have many little twists and turns. In general you're just working your way over to 2nd St. using the least congested streets.

Head northwest on NE 10th Ave. **Turn L** onto NE Alpine Ave. **Turn R** onto NE Lafayette Ave. **Turn R** onto NE 5th St.

Turn L onto NE Galloway St.

Turn R onto NE 4th St. **Turn L** onto NE Cowls St.

Turn R onto NE 3rd st **Turn L** onto NE Adams.

Turn R onto NW 2nd St.

0.5 mi **Turn L** onto SW Hill Rd leaving town and heading south on a chip-seal gentle-up road.

2.1 mi **Turn R** onto SW Peavine Rd.

3.4 mi head west (still on Peavine Rd).

3.7 mi **Turn Slight L** onto SW Youngberg Hill Rd. You'll see Youngberg Bed and Breakfast / Winery on your right, up a steep lane.

5.5 mi **Turn R** onto Masonville Rd (*you'll see the signs to **Coeur de Terre winery** at the intersection of Masonville Rd. and Muddy River up Eagle Point Rd, which is gravel*).

7.2 mi **Turn L** onto SW Muddy Valley Rd.

10.8 mi **Maysara Winery** (15765 SW Muddy Valley Rd, McMinnville, OR 97128).

The sign to Maysara Winery is small. Look for it on the left. The tasting room isn't visible from the road. Turn onto the gravel lane which is packed-down enough that the ride is manageable. The lane does some twists and passes outbuildings before you get to the tasting room. The tasting room and winery were new in 2012.

Back out on Muddy Valley Road **Turn L** to continue. (*You'll see the sign for **Coleman Wines**, SW Lathum Rd.*).

11.2 mi brings you to the highway (Hwy 18, Salmon River Highway).

If you are hungry, there are two cafes along here. There is also a little glass art shop and Laurence Art gallery.

Cross the highway to Bellevue Rd (Hwy 153). *There is no signage indicating street name.*

Bellevue Rd is a quiet little road that winds around with a few ups and downs.

11.9 mi **Turn L** onto SW Delashmutt Ln.
15.2 mi **Turn L** onto busy Hwy 18 (Salmon River Highway) for 351 feet then **Turn R** on to Oldsville Rd.

Farmer Johns. Not only is it a farm stand, it also sells strawberry shortcake (in season) and all manner of ice cream concoctions: shakes, smoothies, cones…

15.5 mi Oldsville Rd. continues onto SW McCabe Chapel Rd.
17 mi **Turn L** onto SW Masonville Rd. and head SE.
18.9 mi **Turn L** onto SW old Sheridan Rd. This road runs parallel to Hwy 18 for a ways.

From here you could rejoin SW Peavine Rd and then **Turn R** onto SW Hill Rd. and retrace your path back to your starting point, OR…

24.1 mi **Turn L** onto SW Cypress Ln.
25.2 **Turn R** onto W 2nd St.
26.2 **Turn L** onto NW Adams St.
Turn R onto NE 3rd St.
Turn L onto NE Baker St.
Turn R onto NE 5th St. which makes a "jog" (becoming 7th St).

26.9 **Turn R** to Alpine Ave.

27.1 **Turn L** onto E 10th to your start/finish point. Walk over a few blocks to **Dominio IV winery** at 888 NE 8th. St. McMinnville.

Eyrie Vineyard (Certified Sustainable and Organic)
Dundee Hills AVA
935 NE 10th Ave, McMinnville, OR 97128
503-472-6315
www.eyrievineyards.com

Hours: 12 p.m.- 5 p.m. daily

Tasting fee: Varies depending on flight chosen. Fee refundable with $60 purchase

Owner/Winemaker: Jason Lett

Production: 10,000 cases/year

About: Founded in 1966, Eyrie holds the distinction of producing the first American Pinot Noir to compete successfully with the renowned Pinot Noirs of Burgundy in Paris in 1979. David Lett, its founder and one of the "vineyard pioneers," is also credited with bringing Pinot Gris to the Pacific Northwest. He and a handful of other hardy souls founding vineyards in Oregon can also be credited with the development and adoption of many of Oregon's wine industry regulations, among them a law, still the most stringent in the U.S., which specifies that Oregon wine must contain 90 percent of the grape indicated by the label.

Jason Lett, David's son, has led the winery since 2005.

Wines

Pinot Noir, Pinot Gris, Pinot Blanc, Melon De Bourgogne, Chardonnay, Muscat Ottonel

Tasting Notes

Muscat Ottonel, one of my favorites, has lots of flowery notes but is still wonderfully dry

The Pinot Noir is lighter than many Pinots, with lots of cherry, red raspberries, spices, and black pepper.

Maysara Winery
(Biodynamic, Demeter Certified)
McMinnville AVA
15765 SW Muddy Valley Rd, McMinnville, OR
97128 503-843-1234
www.maysara.com

Hours: 12 p.m. - 4 p.m. Monday-Saturday
Tasting Fee: $10, waived with purchase of wine
Production: 13,000-18,000 cases/year
Owner: Moe & Flora Montazi
Wine maker: Tahmiene Montazi

About: The vineyard was purchased in 1997 and the first vintage was 2001. The winery is very much a family operation. Moe and Flora are involved with all aspects of operations. Their three daughters are also integral to the business. Tahmiene is the winemaker; Naseem is in charge of sales and marketing; and Hanna is in charge of sales in Oregon, as well as managing foundations associated with the company. The wines are fermented with native yeast (on the grapes from the vineyard) and are mostly unfiltered and unfined.

Moe has been quoted by Katherine Cole (Voodoo Vintners) as saying that the biodynamic approach to farming predates Rudolph Steiner by hundreds of years in his native Persia.

<u>Wines</u>

White: Pinot Gris, Pinot Blanc, Rosè (Pinot Noir), Riesling
Red: Pinot Noirs (six different kinds)

<u>Tasting Notes</u>

All of the wines carry names significant to Persian history. You'll enjoy reading the tasting notes.

I found each of the wines to have wonderful taste profiles. I particularly enjoyed the 2009 Asha Pinot Noir. It was full of red fruit and cherries, some almonds and a bit of smokiness.

McMinnville Loop

A. Farmer Johns

B. Maysara Winery, 15765 SW Muddy Valley Rd, McMinnville OR 97128

C. Eyrie Winery, NE 935,10th Ave McMinnville, OR 97128

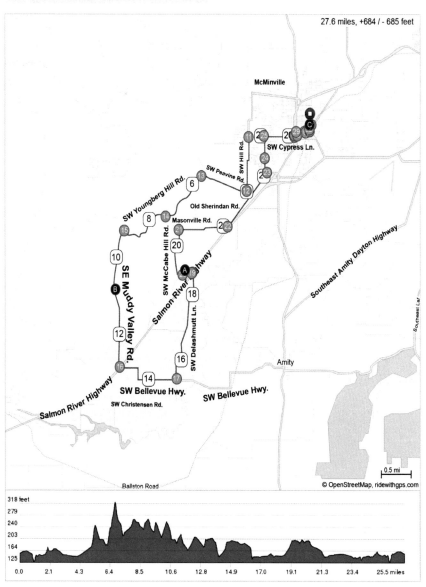

Mcminnville Loop

0.0	0.0	□	Start of route
0.0	0.0	→	From starting point, (close to Eyrie Winery, Turn R onto NE Alpine Ave and begin working your way to 2nd ave
0.2	0.1	←	NE Alpine Ave turns L and becomes NE 7th Ave
0.2	0.0	→	R onto NE Lafayette Ave
0.2	0.0	→	R onto NE 5th St
0.4	0.2	←	L onto NE Galloway St
0.4	0.0	→	R onto NE 4th St
0.7	0.2	←	L onto NE Cowls St
0.7	0.0	→	R onto NE 3rd St
0.8	0.1	←	L onto NW Adams St
0.9	0.1	→	R onto W 2nd St

0.9 miles. +7/-11 feet

2.4	1.5	←	L onto SW Hill Rd S
4.0	1.6	→	R onto SW Peavine Rd
5.6	1.6	←	Slight L onto SW Youngberg Hill Rd
7.4	1.8	→	Slight R onto SW Masonville Rd
9.2	1.8	←	L onto SW Muddy Valley Rd. Watch for Maysara Winery. Driveway on L. Unable to see winery from road. Gravel driveway winds around past some out-buildings to winery On leaving L back onto Muddy Rd.
13.2	4.0	↑	Cross Hwy 18 and Continue onto OR-153 E/SW Bellevue Hwy

12.3 miles. +516/-486 feet

15.3	2.1	←	L onto SW Delashmutt Ln
18.6	3.3	←	L onto OR-18 W/Salmon River Hwy
18.7	0.1	→	R onto SW Oldsville Rd
19.0	0.3	↑	Continue onto SW McCabe Chapel Rd
20.5	1.5	→	R onto SW Masonville Rd
22.1	1.7	←	L onto SW Old Sheridan Rd
24.1	2.0	←	L onto SW Cypress Ln
24.6	0.4	↑	Continue onto S Cypress St
25.2	0.6	→	R onto W 2nd St
26.2	1.0	←	L onto NW Adams St
26.2	0.1	→	R onto NE 3rd St
26.3	0.1	←	L onto NE Baker St

13.1 miles. +179/-218 feet

26.4	0.1	→	R onto NE 5th St
26.8	0.4	←	L onto NE Lafayette Ave
26.9	0.0	←	L onto NE 7th Ave
26.9	0.0	→	NE 7th Ave turns R and becomes NE Alpine Ave
27.1	0.1	←	L onto E 10th Ave back to your start/finish point
27.1	0.1	□	End of route

0.8 miles. +5/-6 feet

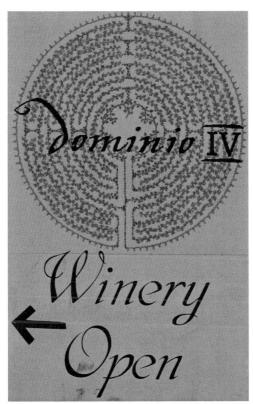

6 AMITY LOOP

This ride does some climbing but rewards you with wonderful down-hills. The route takes you past small farms, vineyards and a neighborhood of gentleman farms. It includes Willamette Valley Cheese Company, (also included in the Salem loop), and Brooks winery. Total distance is about 24 miles.

* See end of chapter for notes on Wheatland Ferry.

Established in the mid-1800's Amity took its name from a school that was built cooperatively by two rival communities. With only a little more than 1,600 people, Amity hasn't seen the growth spurt of some of the other valley towns in Oregon. It does have a quaint "newish" restaurant called **The Blue Goat,** with a menu built around local and fresh produce, fruit and meats. But mostly Amity has the basics: a small grocery, diner, post office, gas station.

In the town of Amity, parking is generally not a problem. Begin on 3rd Street and head south to Nursery Ave.

Turn L at Nursery Ave. Wind your way through the hills, past farms and wooded areas.

4.7 mi **Turn R** onto Lafayette Hwy.
6.8 mi **Turn R** onto Hopewell Rd NW.
mi **Turn R** onto Wallace Rd (SE Dayton-Salem Hwy).

1.1 mi **Willamette Valley Chee**se (8105 Wallace RD NW, Salem 97304).

Retrace your route…

1.2 mi Return to Hopewell Rd NW.
13.8 mi **Turn L** onto Lafayette Hwy.
16 mi **Turn L** onto Hood View Rd and begin to ride uphill.
16.6 **mi Turn slight R,** Hood View Rd joins Eola Hills Rd, the climb becomes steeper.

(If you need to stop for a breather, use it for an excuse to look behind you out over the valley to Mt Hood).

Brooks Winery is on the left. Watch for Cherry Blossom Lane on your left. You can see the Tasting Room from here.

The climb continues only a little more as you leave the winery. Though you will see only the occasional car or truck, take care as you descend the winding road and begin to gain speed. The road passes under a canopy of deciduous trees. The hillside falls away on the right, although unfortunately the trees prevent much of a view.

22.1 mi. Eola Hills Rd ends at the bottom of the hill. **Turn R** onto Old Bethel Rd.
23 mi **Turn L** back to Nursery Ave.
23.7 mi **Turn R** back to Trade Street (3rd St) and your starting point.

This ride can be shortened considerably by not including Willamette Valley Cheese Company. It then becomes a total of 13.2 miles.

Willamette Valley Cheese Company
(Certified Organic Pasture and Production Facilities)
8105 Wallace Rd, NW Salem, OR 97304
503-399-9806
www.wvcheeseco.com

Hours: 10 a.m.- 5 p.m., Tuesday - Saturday
Owner: Rod Volbeda
Cost: Varies

Cheeses are all-natural and hand-crafted from raw or pasteurized Jersey milk. There are no herbicides, pesticides or commercial fertilizers used on the pastures, nor are there any additives, preservatives or hormones in the product itself.

Rod makes 31 different cheeses. What you find in the tasting room depends on what is available that day. Varieties include cheddar and Fontina, Gouda, Havarti, Jack, and Brie.

The day we visited, we found fresh creamy cheese curds that made a delicious snack for the rest of the ride.

Brooks Winery
(Biodynamic, Demeter Certified)
21101 SE Cherry Blossom Lane, Amity, OR 97101
503-435-1278
www.brookswine.com

Hours: 11 a.m. – 5 p.m. Tuesday-Sunday.
Tasting Fee: $10, waived with purchase.
Production: Between 10,000-11,000 cases/ year
Owner: Pascal Brooks, managed by Janie Brooks.
Winemaker: Chris Williams.

About: Founded in 1998, Brooks has one of the more poignant stories connected to the local wineries.

Jimi Brooks, its charismatic founder, was one of the leaders of the biodynamic farming method in vineyards here in the Willamette Valley. His enthusiasm influenced others to embrace the approach. His passion was the vineyards, and the wine he made. He had great plans for his young son Pascal to be a part of this dream, but in 2004, at just 38 years old, Jimi died suddenly from an aortic aneurism, only weeks before that year's harvest.

Through the generosity and friendship of the Oregon wine community, not only were Brooks' grapes harvested and fermented, but legal arrangements were made that allowed eight-year-old Pascal to become sole owner of the winery with his aunt, Janie Brooks Heuck, acting as manager. The winery has since thrived, and in 2014 moved to its present location near the top of Eola Hills.

Wines

There are an astonishing number of white wines in the Brooks' repertoire.

> **White**: Two Gewürztraminers, dry Muscat, Pinot Blanc, Rosé (Pinot Gris), and four Rieslings, each a different vineyard, and slightly different style.
> **Red**: Seven Pinot Noirs

Tasting Notes

We loved the dry whites. The Muscat (2009 Terue Dry Muscat) was our favorite, full of floral notes and a little citrus. From the nose it seemed like it would be sweet, but instead it was delightfully dry.

* Wheatland Ferry: If you're coming from Portland, you might consider taking I-5 South to the Gervais exit. You will save a significant amount of driving time. For information call 503-588-7979 or visit www.wheatlandferry.com.

The Bicycling Wine Tourist

Amity Loop

A.   Willamette Valley Cheese Factory   B.   Brooks Winery

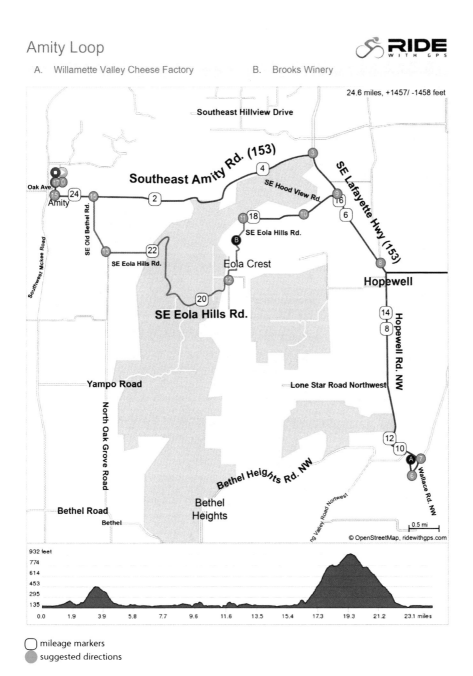

24.6 miles, +1457/ -1458 feet

mileage markers

suggested directions

Amity Loop

0.0	0.0	☐	Start of route
0.1	0.1	←	from School on 3rd Street L onto Oak Ave
0.3	0.2	←	L onto Nursery St SE
4.9	4.5	→	R onto OR-153 E/OR-154 S/SE Lafayette Hwy
6.9	2.1	→	R onto Hopewell Rd NW
10.7	3.8	→	Sharp R onto gravel driveway to Willamette Valley Cheese Factory
11.1	0.4	←	Sharp L back onto OR-221 N/Wallace Rd NW
11.4	0.3	←	L onto Hopewell Rd NW and retrace path until arriving Hood View Rd

11.4 miles. +569/-577 feet

14.8	3.4	←	L onto OR-153 W/OR-154 N/SE Lafayette Hwy
16.1	1.3	←	L onto SE Hood View Rd
17.2	1.1	→	Slight R onto SE Eola Hills Rd
18.2	1.0	←	L to stay on SE Eola Hills Rd watch for entrance to Brooks Winery on L
19.4	1.2	→	R to stay on SE Eola Hills Rd
22.8	3.4	→	R onto SE Old Bethel Rd
23.7	0.9	←	L onto OR-153 W/SE Amity Rd
24.3	0.6	→	R onto Oak Ave
24.5	0.2	→	R onto 3rd St. back to your start/finish point
24.6	0.0	☐	End of route

13.2 miles. +929/-924 feet

7 Dallas Oregon Loop

This ride begins at the Dallas Aquatic Center and includes Illahe and Johan Wineries. It is a loop that passes through the Basket Slough Natural Reserve, a habitat for waterfowl. The roads through the slough are gravel but basically flat.

This ride has the least amount of elevation of any of the rides in this collection. Total distance is about 30 miles.

Dallas, the county seat of Polk County is situated on the north side of Rickreall Creek, about 15 miles west of Salem, and has a population of about 16,000. Historically it won the honor for Polk county seat when citizens raised $17,000 to build a branch of the narrow gauge railroad (built from 1878-80). Originally named Cynthiana, the town became Dallas through the curious logic that since George Mifflin Dallas was vice president under James K. Polk, for whom the county was named, "Dallas" was a natural choice for the town.

Where to eat: Dallas has the usual franchises (e.g. Subway and Quiznos) for sandwiches. There's also a Safeway with a deli that will make you a sandwich.

This ride starts at the Aquatic Center, which is set in a park. There's plenty of free parking. On leaving the lot, turn right onto SE Lacreole Dr.

0.2 mi **Turn L** onto SE Miller Ave. 0.5 mi **Turn R.** onto SE Godsey Rd.

1.1 mi **Turn L.** onto Clow Corner Rd/SE Monmouth Cut Off Rd. 2.4

mi **Turn R.** onto Ballard Rd. (gravel).

3.6 mi Watch for **Illahe Winery** driveway (gravel), which winds up to the winery past the vineyard.

5.0 mi On leaving, retrace path to Clow Corner Rd and **Turn R.**

6.8 mi **Turn L** onto Riddel Rd.

7.7 mi Continue onto Orrs Corner Rd.

9.1 mi Continue onto Bowersville Rd (gravel). 10 mi **Turn L** onto Ellendale Ave.

11.1 mi **Turn R** onto N. Fir Villa Rd. (soon becomes gravel). Does some twisting.

13.4 mi **Turn R** onto NE Kings Valley Hwy, cross highway onto Smithfield Rd (no sign) and immediately **Turn R** onto Coville Rd. (gravel). Stay on this road as you ride through the Basket Slough Reserve.

16.9 mi **Turn L** onto OR 99W / Pacific Hwy. Watch for Entrance to **Johan Vineyard**. Shares entrance with Left Bank Winery. At the split, continue to the right. Driveway becomes gravel and is somewhat steep in places.

On leaving **Turn R** back onto Pacific Hwy. Highway can be busy but the shoulders are clean and ample.

24.1 mi **Turn R** onto Rickreall Rd.

25 mi Rickreall Rd joins Hwy 223. As you get closer to Dallas the road becomes Ellendale.

27.7 mi **Turn L** onto SE Lacreole Dr. There is a signal light and a left-turn lane.

28.4 mi **Turn R.** into Aquatic Center parking lot, your start/finish point.

Illahe Vineyards and Winery
(LIVE-Certified, sustainable practices)
Willamette Valley AVA
3275 Ballard Rd., Dallas, OR 97338
503-831-1248
www.illahevineyard.com

Hours: (Summer) 11 a.m. – 4 p.m. Thursday - Saturday
Tasting Fee: $5, waived with purchase.
Production: 4,000 cases/year.
Owners: Lowell and Pauline Ford
Winemaker: Brad Ford

About: Illahe's grapes were sold to other vintners until the winery was built in 2008, and the first Estate bottling was crafted. Sustainable practices include: gravity-fed vinification, solar power and rainwater harvesting. An additional practice includes using horses to mow the weeds and during harvest to bring the grapes from the vineyard to the sorting table.

<u>Wines</u>

Half of Illahe's production is Pinot Noir, the other half is Viognier, Riesling, Grüner Veltliner, and Tempranillo.

<u>Tasting Notes</u>

Among our favorites was the Viognier, with its mineral freshness and traditional notes of flowers, lychees and pears. The Pinot Noir was also excellent. Of the available vintages, the 2008 Reserve won our vote. Even though it had big bold fruit flavors, there was the hint of leather and tobacco with enough tannin to give it depth.

Johan Vineyards
(Biodynamic Demeter Certified) Willamette Valley AVA
4285 N. Paci ic Hwy (99W), Rickreall, OR 97371
866-379-6029
www.johanvineyards.com

Hours: 11 a.m. – 5 p.m. daily
Tasting Fee: $5. One fee refundable with each purchase.
Production: 2000-3000 cases/year
Owner: Dag Sundby
Winemaker/Viticulturist: Dan Rinke

About: The owner, Dag Sundby, arrived here from Norway with the express purpose of having a vineyard and making wine. He hired Dan Rinke, a biodynamic advocate who has produced a mix of classic and beautifully nuanced wines.

Wines

Pinot Noir, Chardonnay, Pinot Gris, Vin Gris (Pinot Noir Rosé), Grüner Veltliner.

All wines are estate grown, produced and bottled.

Tasting Notes

The Pinot Gris was aromatic and complex from spending six months on the lees (spent yeast hulls) in neutral oak. It had a citrus twist at the end that made it very refreshing and satisfying.

Of the Pinot Noirs, I favored the 2008 Nils Reserve, a classic Pinot with flavors from beginning to end, full of dark fruit, spice and earth.

dallas, loop

A. johan vineyard and winery   B. illahe vineyard and winery

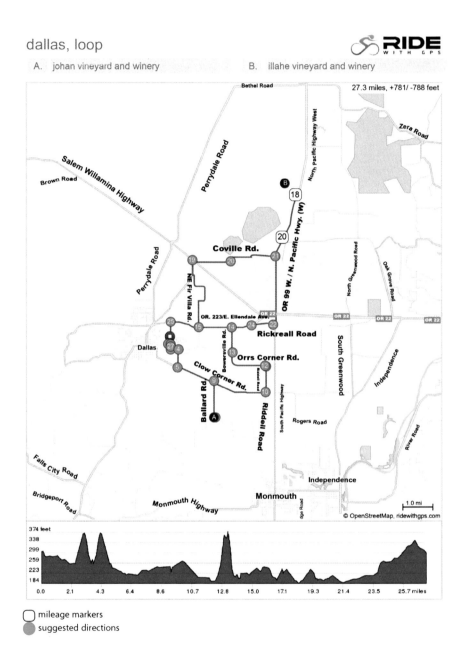

◯ mileage markers
⬤ suggested directions

Dallas Loop

1.	0.0	⚑	Start of route
2.	0.1	→	As you leave the aquatic center, R onto SE Lacreole Dr
3.	0.3	←	L onto SE Miller Ave
4.	0.5	→	R onto SE Godsey Rd
5.	1.1	←	L onto Clow Corner Rd/SE Monmouth Cut Off Rd
6.	2.4	→	R onto Ballard Rd. (Gravel)
7.	3.6	→	R to stay on Ballard Rd. Watch for Illahe Driveway (gravel, winds uphill
8.	3.8	←	L to stay on Ballard Rd
9.	4.9	→	R onto Clow Corner Rd/SE Monmouth Cut Off Rd
10.	6.8	←	L onto Riddell Rd

6.8 miles. +262/-349 feet

11.	7.6	←	Keep L to stay on Riddell Rd
12.	7.7	↑	Continue onto Orrs Corner Rd
13.	9.1	↑	Continue onto Bowersville Rd (gravel)
14.	10.0	←	L onto OR-223 S/E Ellendale Ave
15.	11.1	→	R onto N Fir Villa Rd. (Soon becomes gravel)
16.	13.3	←	L to stay on N Fir Villa Rd
17.	13.4	→	R onto NE Kings Valley Hwy
18.	13.9	↑	Continue onto Smithfield Rd, (briefly)
19.	13.9	→	Sharp R onto Coville Rd, (gravel)
20.	15.4	→	R to stay on Coville Rd

8.7 miles. +292/-274 feet

21.	16.9	←	L onto OR-99W N/N Pacific Hwy W. Watch for Entrace to Johan Vineyard. Shares entrance with L Bank Winery. On leaving, R back onto 99W
22.	24.1	→	R onto Rickreall Rd
23.	25.0	→	R to stay on Rickreall Rd
24.	25.0	←	L onto OR-223 S/Rickreall Rd (signs for State Hwy 223/Dallas)
25.	27.7	←	L onto SE Lacreole Dr
26.	28.4	→	R onto SE Walnut Ave, your start/finish point
27.	28.5	⚑	End of route

13.1 miles. +322/-231 feet

8
SALEM LOOP

This ride includes Cristom and Bethel Heights Winery, and Willamette Cheese Factory. It can be ridden any number of ways. You might consider visiting the cheese factory first, giving you a snack as you taste the wines. This will mean some doubling back. Total distance is about 22 miles. Overall this ride has some hills alternating with quiet country roads. There is a two mile section of gravel.

*See note at the end of this chapter regarding ferry information.

Salem, Oregon's capital and county seat of Marion County, is located in the middle of the Willamette Valley. The Willamette River runs alongside the town. Established in 1842, Salem became the state capital in 1851 as well as home to two universities, Willamette and Corban. Its population of 154,600 makes Salem Oregon's third largest town. There's a sizeable downtown with some major chain stores, and as with any town this size, you may have to ask directions to find what you're looking for.

Where to eat: There are many fast food franchises along Wallace Rd. In town **Wild Pear** (372 State St, Salem, OR 97301) has a tasty and highly recommended sack lunch menu. The day I visited there was a line of people waiting for a table, and yet, my sandwich and chips were ready, and I was out the door in 15 minutes. Their hours are 10 a.m. - 5:30 p.m. Monday-Saturday.

The ride starts in a little park at the corner of Doaks Ferry and Brush College Rd NW (Brush College Park).

Out of the park, **Turn R** onto Doaks Ferry Rd. and ride through a suburban neighborhood until reaching Wallace Rd (OR 221 North / Salem-Dayton Hwy).

0.4 mi **Turn L** onto Wallace Rd. This road can be busy and has narrowing shoulders as you get out of town.
3.5 mi At the little town of Lincoln (gas station, convenience store) **Turn**
L onto Zena Rd. From here to Bethel Heights Vineyard it's mostly uphill. 7.4 mi **Turn R** onto Bethel Heights Rd. This road isn't marked well, but the blue winery sign on Zena Rd as you approach gives you the best indication that you're on the right path.
7.9 mi **Turn R** onto gravel driveway (0.2 mi to parking lot for **Bethel Heights** tasting room).
8.2 **Turn R. when leaving winery,** road becomes gravel at 9.0 mi. and continues for 2 miles.
12.1 **Turn L** onto Spring Valley Rd.
12.9 mi **Turn R.** onto Hopewell Rd.
13 mi **Turn R** onto Wallace Rd.
13.3 **Turn R** into gravel driveway to **Willamette Cheese Factory**. Retrace path to Hopewell (**L** onto Wallace, **L** onto Hopewell).
13.7 mi **Turn L** onto Spring Valley Rd, there are some rolling hills.
16.5 mi **Turn R** into a short gravel driveway to **Cristom Vineyard.** Return to Spring Valley Rd and **Turn L.**
18 mi Cross Zena Road. **Turn R** and curve around a picturesque little white church with a steeple as the road becomes Brush College Rd. It's mostly downhill from here to the intersection of Doaks Ferry.
1.8 mi. **Turn L** onto Doakes Ferry and **Turn R.** into Brush College Park, the starting/ending point.

Cristom Vineyards
(Sustainable, LIVE Certified)
Eola-Amity Hills AVA
6905 Spring Valley Rd., NW Salem, OR 97304

503-375-3068
www.cristomwine.com

Hours: 11 a.m. – 5 p.m. daily, closed Mondays
Tasting Fee: $10, waived with $50 purchase
Production: 15,000 cases/year
Owners: Paul Gerrie
Winemaker: Steve Doerner

About: The Gerrie family has been making wine at Cristom since 1992 with the same winemaker and the same vineyard manager. Their approach, like many of the wineries featured in these rides, utilizes native yeast, which is what's on the grapes as they arrive from the field.

Wines

> **White:** Pinot Gris, Viognier, Chardonnay
> **Red:** There are four Pinot Noirs and usually three Cuvées

There are four Pinot Noir blocks in the vineyard, each named for a different woman in the family's history. The wine made from each block carries that woman's name and image. The Cuvées are made from a combination of the various blocks.

Tasting Notes

Of the Pinot Noirs, my vote went to Cristom Louise, which was full of dark fruit, black cherries, raspberries and plums. There were also hints of chocolate and it had a wonderful soft mouthfeel.

The Pinot Gris and Viognier both had good acidity and mineral notes. We bought a bottle of Pinot Gris and added it to our picnic out on the deck.

Bethel Heights Vineyard
(Sustainable, LIVE Certified)
Eola-Amity Hills AVA
6060 Bethel Heights Rd., NW Salem, OR 97304
503-581-2262

www.bethelheights.com

Hours: 11 a.m. – 5 p.m. Tue-Sun. Closed Monday
Tasting Fee: $5, waived with wine purchase
Production: 13,000 cases/year
Owners: Jessie and Jon Casteel Winemaker: Ben Casteel

About: Bethel Heights Vinyard was started by two couples, twin brothers and their wives. They, working in academia, decided they wanted the "idyllic" life of growing grapes and making wine. And no, they'll tell you, it hasn't all been idyllic. They were some of the first pioneers to start vineyards in 1977. The winery itself was established in 1984.

Wines

> **Whites**: Chardonnay, Riesling, and Pinot Blanc.
> **Reds**: Pinot Noir from various blocks, each with its own nuance.

Tasting Notes

<u>Tasting Notes</u>

The day we visited, the wines were stellar, as usual.

My favorite red wine was a Pinot from the west block that was full of cherries and black currants, a hint of vanilla, and enough tannin to give it character.

The wine that always gets my vote at this winery, though, is the unoaked Chardonnay. It had bright, crisp minerality and tasted of green apples and citrusy lemon – wonderful on a warm summer afternoon.

Willamette Valley Cheese Company (Certified Organic Pasture and Production Facilities)
8105 Wallace Rd. NW Salem, OR 97304
503-399-9806
www.wvcheeseco.com

Hours: 10 a.m. – 5 p.m., Tuesday - Saturday.
Owner: Rod Volbeda

About: The cheeses are all-natural and hand-crafted from raw or pasteurized Jersey milk. There are no herbicides, pesticides or commercial fertilizers used on the pastures. There are also no product additives, preservatives or hormones.

Rod makes 31 different cheeses. What you find in the tasting room depends on what is available Varieties include cheddar and Fontina, Gouda, Havarti, Jack, and Brie.

The day we were there, we found creamy cheese curds that made delicious snacks for the rest of the ride.

*Wheatland Ferry:

- If you are driving down from Portland to do this ride, you might consider taking the Wheatland Ferry, and driving south on Wallace Rd. to Doaks Ferry Rd. to Brush College Park.

- Call or check the website to see whether the Wheatland Ferry is running. 503-588-7979 / www.wheatlandferry.com

- The ferry charges $1.00 for bicyclists.

Salem Loop

A. Bethel Heights vineyard and winery

B. Willamette Valley Cheese

C. Christom Vineyards and Winery

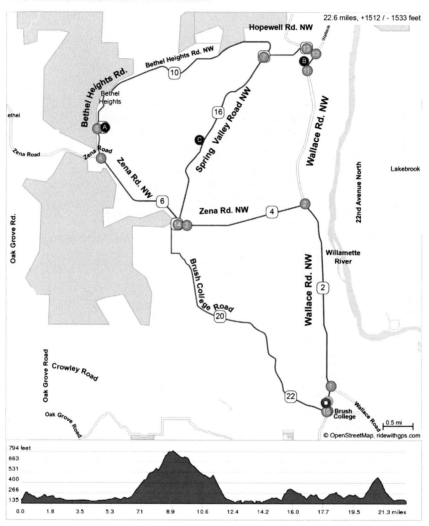

mileage markers
suggested directions

Salem Loop

0.0	0.0	▢	Start of route
0.4	0.4	←	R as you leave Brush College City Park onto Doaks Ferry.Turn L onto OR-221 N, (Wallace Rd)
3.4	3.0	←	L onto Zena Rd NW
5.5	2.0	→	Slight R to stay on Zena Rd NW
7.4	1.9	→	R onto Bethel Heights Rd NW.
7.9	0.5	→	R into gravel driveway for Bethel Hts Winery
8.1	0.2	→	R back onto Bethel Heights Rd NW. Road become gravel for 2mi until reaching Spring Valley Rd.
12.0	3.9	←	Sharp L onto Spring Valley Rd NW

12.0 miles. +941/-913 feet

12.8	0.8	←	L onto Hopewell Rd NW
13.0	0.2	→	R onto OR-221 S/Wallace Rd NW
13.3	0.3	→	Sharp R into gravel driveway to Willamette valley Cheese Company.
13.5	0.3	←	Sharp L to return to OR-221 N/Wallace Rd NW
13.8	0.3	←	L back onto Hopewell Rd NW
14.0	0.2	←	L onto Spring Valley Rd NW Watch for gravel driveway on R to Cristom Vineyards. On leaving, R back onto Spring Valley Rd NW

2.0 miles. +82/-82 feet

18.0	4.0	→	Cross Zena Rd.Turn R onto Brush College Rd NW. Follow back to Doaks Ferry. L and then R into park. Back to start/finsh point
22.6	4.6	▢	End of route

8.6 miles. +386/-434 feet

9 COLUMBIA GORGE LOOP

This ride begins about six miles east of the toll bridge from Hood River. It includes Syncline and Domaine Pouillon wineries, as well as Memaloose Tasting Room. It has beautiful scenery throughout. There is some climbing. Total distance is about 16.5 miles.

Hood River, population 7,200 is situated in the Columbia River Gorge at the foot of Mt. Hood, surrounded by fields, orchards, and vineyards. Spring, summer, and fall, visitors and residents alike enjoy hiking as well as bicycling. On the Columbia River, water sports include wind surfing, sailing, swimming and more. With Mt. Hood so close-by, Hood River truly is a year-round sports enthusiast's heaven.

The Toll Bridge over the Columbia River is closed to pedestrians and bicycles. If you are without a vehicle, you can try hitching a ride with a pickup, or something similar. The toll is $1.00 (each way) for passenger vehicles.

If you are driving you may want to get your gas in Oregon, so you don't have to pump it yourself.

You pass through **Bingen, WA,** after crossing the toll bridge from Hood River. Established in 1892, Bingen has a population of around 700. There are a handful of businesses, as well as some places to eat on Highway 14, which runs through town.

All of the wineries that are included in this ride are technically part of **Lyle, WA**. With just over 500 people, Lyle is a sleepy little town. It does, however, have the basics: post office, little grocery store, and a gas station.

Where to eat. Your best options for food may be in Hood River. There are numerous little cafes and sandwich shops along Oak Street. A little wandering around will show you more.

After you cross the toll bridge, **Turn R** and continue through Bingen on Hwy 14 until you see Old Hwy 8, a road on the left. This is about 6 miles from the toll bridge
Turn L on Old Hwy 8 at Rowland Lake. There is parking just off Hwy 14 (*The mileage counter starts from here*).
There is more parking as you drive up Old Hwy 8 just around the bend of the lake. The route is a gentle up with the rock cliffs on the left and to the right the lake and beyond that the Columbia River. Most of the way to the first winery, Syncline, there are views of the river and of Mt. Hood.
3.2 mi. **Turn L** at the intersection of Balch Rd and Sauter Rd. onto Balch Rd. You will see the sign for **Syncline** from the intersection. The driveway is graveled but short.
On leaving Syncline, return to the highway and **Turn L**. The road is somewhat hilly. You will pass other small wineries on the way to Domaine Pouillon.
5.1 mi **Turn L** at the intersection of Old Hwy 8 and Canyon Rd. (you'll see the sign to Appleton and Domaine Poullion).
5.5 mi **Turn L**. The road forks into Snowden Rd. From here to Domaine Poullion there is a winding climb. The pavement is good and there is the occasional shade from huge oak trees along the way.
7.3 mi **Turn R** into gates at **Domaine Poullion.**
Turn L on leaving Domaine Poullion, and retrace your route

to Canyon Rd. From the winery to the main highway is mostly an exhilarating downhill ride. The traffic is light but there are no shoulders so give care as you descend.

11.4 mi Turn L at the intersection of Canyon and Hwy 14 (Lewis and Clark Hwy). The highway is busy and noisy, but as soon as you cross the bridge into Lyle, you will see the **Memaloose Tasting** room on the right. The tasting room shares the building (and the sign) with NW Real Estate.

To return to your car it is simplest to take the main highway. Yes, it's noisy, but there is ample shoulder.

Turn L onto the highway, re-cross the bridge and continue west. The Columbia River is on the left and the rugged rock cliffs on your right. 4.6 mi brings you back to Rowland Lake and your starting point for a total of about 16.5 miles

Syncline
(Biodynamic, Demeter Certified)
Columbia Gorge AVA
111 Balch Road, Lyle, WA 98635
509- 365 4361
www.synclinewine.com

Hours: 11 a.m.–6 p.m. Thursday Sunday (Feb.-Nov.)
Tasting Fee: $5, waived with purchase
Owners: James Mantone and his wife Poppie. James is both vineyard manager and winemaker.
Production: 5,000 cases/year

About: The winery opened in 1999 with 76 cases of Pinot Noir. There is talk James is going to be training the horses to plow his grapevines. Grapes are sourced from these and other like-minded vineyards.

Wines

The winery specializes in Rhone varietals.

White: Roussane, Grüner Veltliner, Viognier, various blends
Red: Mourvedre, Grenache, Syrah

Tasting Notes

The white wines hadn't yet been released when we paid a visit. Our favorites among of the reds included:

- Mourvedre 2010, which tasted of blackberries, a twist of blueberry and white pepper.
- Genache 2010 had a wonderful mouthfeel, and was full of plum, and black berries, spice notes and black pepper.

The tasting room part of the winery can be noisy, depending on what part of winemaking is happening in the background.

Domaine Pouillon
(Biodynamic Demeter Certified)
Columbia Gorge AVA
170 Lyle-Snowden Road, Lyle, WA 98635
509- 365 2795
www.domainepouillon.com

Hours: 12 p.m. – 5 p.m. Friday - Sunday
Tasting Fee: $5, waived with purchase
Production: 4,000 cases/year
Owner/Manager: Alexis Pouillon and his wife, Juliet
Winemaker: Alexis Pouillon

About: This winery opened in 2007. Alexis Pouillon apprenticed in Chateauneuf, France, and has been involved with winemaking since 1994. Both Alexis and Juliet are involved in all aspects of this winery today. The Pouillon vineyard is very small (about two acres), so additional grapes are sourced from other like-minded vineyards.

The tasting room is a comfortable but minimalist space above the winery. You'll see it as you turn into the driveway. It has wonderful French touches, such as small, cut-glass chandeliers, as well as some upholstered chairs and a Persian rug. There is also a small outside patio.

<u>Wines</u>

Syrah, Gewurztraminer, and in the European tradition, four to five exquisite blends, both red and white. The wines are un-fined.

<u>Tasting Notes</u>

Among our favorites was the Deux 2011, a classic blend of Chardonnay and Viognier. The aromas are soft, and the flavors are pears with a twist of tangerine and touch of oak.

Another standout was the Katydid 2010, a blend of Grenache, Mourvedre, Syrah, and Cinsaut. This wine is done in a classic Rhone style, and has aromas that begin with raspberries and earth. As you taste this will evolve to chocolate and cassis, and then a twist of black pepper.

Memaloose, (Organic), Columbia Gorge AVA
34 State St. Hwy 14,
(Lewis &Clark Hwy) Lyle,Washington
Zip Code 98635
360-635 2887

www.winesofthegorge.com

Hours:Fri-Sun. 11-5. (Open 7 days in summer).

Tasting fee: $5, waived with purchase.

Production: 2,000cases/year.

Owners: The McCormick family.

Winemaker: Brian McCormick.

About: This winery opened in 2006. The grapes come from the McCormick family vineyard in the Lyle area and from Mosier, Idiot's Grace, owned by Brian. He is both a viticulturist and a vintner. He brings a background of France's Alsace and California's Sonoma Valley to his approach to winemaking. His goal is to show the terroir of the Gorge AVA to its best advantage.

Wines

    White: Riesling, Chardonnay,Various blends
    Red: Cabernet Franc, Primitivo, Pinot Noir Rosé (summer)

Tasting notes:

Our favorites included:
Memaloose Chardonnay, 2010, a classic bright chardonnay flavor soft with apples and pears.

Idiots Grace Primitivo, 2010, A Zinfandel with lots of black fruit, cherries and berries, some spices and a twist of black pepper. Its Columbia Gorge acidity makes it food-friendly.

Gorge Loop

A. Syncline winery, 111 Balch Rd, Lyle, 98635

B. Domaine Pouillon, 170 Lyle-Snowden Rd. Lyle 98635

C. Memaloose Tasting Rm. 34 State St. Lyle 98635

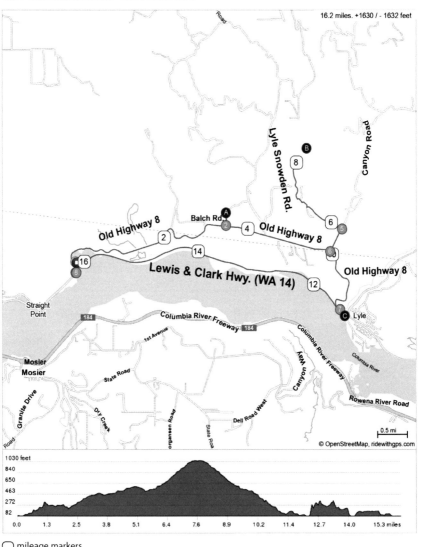

16.2 miles. +1630 / - 1632 feet

◯ mileage markers

⬤ suggested directions

Gorge Loop

0.0	0.0	☐	Start of route
3.3	3.3	←	from parking area L onto Old Hwy 8 and begin a gentle climb.Turn L onto Balch Rd. you can see Syncline Winery from intersection
3.6	0.3	←	L back onto Lyle White Salmon Rdand continue to Canyon Rd.
5.4	1.8	←	L onto Canyon Rd. Sign to Appleton and Domaine Pouillon

5.4 miles. +712/-261 feet

5.8	0.4	←	Slight L onto Lyle Snowden Rd/Snowden Rd Climb up until begins to level out and watch for Domaine Pouillon on R. On leaving L and retrace path to Canyon Rd
9.5	3.7	→	Slight R onto Canyon Rd
9.9	0.4	←	L to stay on Canyon Rd

4.5 miles. +513/-549 feet

11.1	1.2	→	R onto WA-14/Lewis and Clark Hwy and cross bridge. Memaloose Tasting Rm is immediately on R. On leaving L back onto Lewis/Clark Hwy(WA-14) and return to Rowland Lake (approx 4.6 miles) For a total of ~16 miles
16.2	5.1	☐	End of route

6.3 miles. +660/-719 feet

10 Hood River/Mosier Loop

This ride offers two options: an out and back through the Mosier Twin Tunnels or a challenging loop that returns through the tunnels. The out and back choice is a pleasant ride through meadows and forested areas with intermittent views of the Columbia River on the Mark O. Hatfield trail and Highway 30 through Mosier. There is a gradual climb up to Garnier Vineyards. The loop variation includes about 12 miles of dirt/gravel road that is not maintained during the winter. It has significant elevation gains and wonderful views of the valley. The wineries on this ride include Garnier Vineyards in Mosier and Cerulean tasting room in Hood River.

Mosier, population about 430, is situated between Hood River and The Dalles. Orchards and logging were the mainstay of the economy originally. Fruit is still important to Mosier, but with its proximity to all that has contributed to Hood River's growth, tourism is becoming important, as well. The historic Columbia River Highway, designed by Samuel Lancaster and built from 1913-1922, was abandoned when the new interstate highway was built. In 2000 it was restored and reopened as a bicycle/hiking trail. See www.gorgefriends.org for details. In the tunnel, there is graffiti carved into the wood beams that dates back to 1921 when drivers were snowbound for several days.

(Option 1: Out and Back)
(Mileage tables not included for this version.)

At the top of Old Columbia River Drive you'll find the (for fee) parking lot, which is also the trailhead. The paved trail requires a day-use pass for $5, which is dispensed by a yellow self-service machine. There are well-maintained outdoor toilets.

The trail is mostly level and gives you views of the Columbia River now and then. It winds through meadows and forested areas. Total distance is about five miles.

On leaving the tunnels, **Turn L** onto Rock Creek Rd. Follow it to US 30 W / 1st Ave.

6.3 mi **Turn L** onto 1st Ave and ride through Mosier. Continue up the hill (still US 30 W / 1st Ave).

7.6 mi watch for **Garnier Vineyards** on the left. Turn in at the driveway and ride a short distance (gravel) to the tasting room.

To return: Retrace your path back to your car. Total distance is about 15 miles. Head to **Cerulean Tasting Room** (304 Oak Street) in a courtyard in downtown Hood River.

(Option 2: Loop)

For those who need a loop for it to feel like a REAL ride, one is included. However, note that road bikes would hate this route.

I've been over the route multiple times, and the best approach is probably to start on Eastside Rd. in Hood River, as there may be less elevation from this side. There are several free parking areas on Columbia River Drive, close to Hwy 35 S.

This route takes you through the hills between Hood River and Mosier. There are approximately 12 miles of gravel/dirt road. The best time to take this road is in the summer when there has been no rain. It's not maintained the rest of the year. There is also some significant elevation gain (see the map for this ride). The highest point is 2,000 feet.

This is a tough ride, but with the elevation gains there are incredible views to the south. There is also little to no traffic, so you can stop where you please. Pay close attention to your map, though. A GPS might be helpful as the dirt/gravel roads aren't well-marked.

Out of the parking lot Turn L and head down Columbia River Dr. to Hwy 35. **Turn L** onto OR-35. There are signs to Mt. Hood.

0.4 mi **Turn L** onto Eastside Rd.

2.3 mi **Turn L** onto Old Dalles Dr.

4.3 mi **Turn R** onto Elder Rd / Old Dalles Dr. It becomes gravel, which gives way to dirt in places.

10.5 mi the road becomes Huskey Rd. The sign at this "intersection" labels the road you just left as "Elder Road." Be vigilant, Huskey has branches. Stay left at the fork—the right branch comes out on Hwy 35 but south of Hood River.

12 mi (approx.) road becomes paved again.

14.8 mi **Turn L** onto 3rd Ave. You have arrived in Mosier!

14.9 mi **Turn R** onto Idaho St.

15.0 mi **Turn R** onto 1st Ave and head out of town up the hill. Watch for signs indicating **Garnier Vineyard.** Turn into the gravel driveway and continue a short distance to the tasting room.

On leaving, **Turn R** and head down the hill and through Mosier.

17.6 mi Make **slight R** onto Rock Creek Rd.

18.3 mi **Slight R** onto path for Mosier twin tunnels.

22.6 mi Continue onto Mark O. Hatfield Trail.

22.8 mi Go past the parking lot at the trailhead, and continue down Old Columbia River Dr. Follow the switchbacks down to where you parked your car.

Head to **Cerulean Tasting Room** (304 Oak Street) in a courtyard in downtown Hood River.

Garnier Vineyards
(Sustainable farming practices)
Columbia Gorge AVA 8467
US 30, Mosier, OR 97040
541-478-2200
www.gardniervineyards.com

Hours: By appointment only
Tasting Fee: $5, waived with purchase of a bottle of wine
Owner: Tom Garnier
Winemaker: Jerry Dettwiler
Production: 2,500 cases/year

About: After a bad cherry year, the cherry orchard was replaced with grape vines. The first vintage was in 2007. Most of the grapes produced are sold to other wineries.

The tasting room is down a short gravel driveway. It's a rustic little room with a bar, plenty of windows that look down on the vineyard and out on the Columbia River. You'll meet Todd, who is pretty much responsible for everything: tasting room, sales, etc.

Wines

The day I visited there were eight wines to sample.

> **White**: Chardonnay, Viognier, Sauvignon Blanc, Merlot Rosé
> **Red**: Pinot Noir, Merlot, Syrah-Merlot blend, cherry-dessert wine

I thought the Sauvignon Blanc was beautiful and aromatic. There also was a stellar Pinot Noir. For me the stand out was the Merlot – full of fruit, a touch of smokiness and a silky mouthfeel.

Cerulean Wine
(Certified Organic)
Columbia Gorge AVA
304 Oak Street, Hood River, OR 97031
503-705-9840
www.ceruleanwine.com

Hours: noon-6 p.m. Thursday-Sunday
Tasting Fee: 5 pours for $5. One fee waived per bottle purchased.
Owners: Tammy and Jeff Miller
Winemaker: Carey Kientz
Production: 1,500 cases/year

About: This small family-owned winery sources the majority of their grapes from their own (Acadia) vineyard, which is across the river in Washington State.

The owners bought the vineyard in 2007 and by the next year produced their first commercial vintage.
The tasting room is off a courtyard in the center of town. It's a small, tastefully decorated space that lends itself to focusing on the wine.

Wines

>**White**: Pinot Gris, Riesling, Gewürztraminer, Pinot Gris Rosé
>**Red**: Pinot Noir, Barbera, Merlot, Syrah, red blend

A favorite was the Barbera, a medium-bodied wine with a rich red color, lots of blackberries and a pomegranate finish. This wine would go great with pasta dishes!

Hood River/Mosier Loop

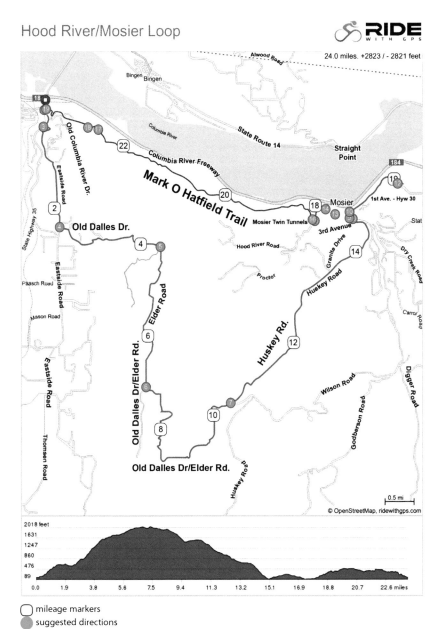

24.0 miles. +2823 / - 2821 feet

mileage markers
suggested directions

Hood River/Mosier Loop

0.0	0.0	▢	Start of route
0.0	0.0	→	out of parking lot located on Old Columbia River Dr. R onto Hwy 35 S
0.1	0.1	←	L onto OR-35 S (signs for Mt Hood/Oregon 35)
0.4	0.3	←	L onto Eastside Rd
2.3	1.9	←	L onto Old Dalles Dr
4.3	2.0	→	R onto Elder Rd/Old Dalles Dr. Road becomes gravel which gives way to dirt in places
6.8	2.5	←	Elder Rd turns slightly L and becomes Old Dalles Dr/Elder Rd

6.8 miles. +2022/-140 feet

10.5	3.6	↑	Continue straight onto Huskey Rd. Be vigilent. at the fork, L (the R loops back to town)
14.8	4.3	←	L onto 3rd Ave
14.9	0.1	→	R onto Idaho St
15.0	0.1	→	R onto 1st Ave
16.1	1.1	←	L into Garnier driveway
16.3	0.2	→	R onto U.S. 30 W/1st Ave and ride through Mosier
17.6	1.3	→	Slight R onto Rock Creek Rd
17.8	0.2	→	R onto Rock Creek Rd
18.3	0.4	→	Slight R onto the path for the Mosier tunnels
18.3	0.1	↑	Continue straight onto Mark O. Hatfield Trail

11.5 miles. +348/-1672 feet

22.6	4.3	↑	Continue straight to stay on Mark O. Hatfield Trail
22.8	0.2	↑	Continue onto Old Columbia River Dr. Down a series of turns to the parking lot, L back to your start/finish point
24.0	1.2	▢	End of route

5.7 miles. +94/-295 feet

RESOURCES

BICYCLE SHOPS/RENTALS

Discover Bicycles
210 State Street
Hood River, OR 97031
541-386-4820
www.discoverbicyles.com
Large fleet of bicycles for rent by the day/week. Call for details.

Tommy's Bicycle Shop
624 NE Third Street
McMinnville, OR 97128
503-472-2010
www.tommysbicycle.net
No rental capacities at the time of this writing. However, you can ship your bike to and from here.

Veloce Bicycles
3202 SE Hawthorne Blvd
Portland, OR 97214
971-279-7725
www.velocebicycles.com
Bikes to rent. Call for
details.

Olson's Bicycles 1904 Elm Street
Forest Grove, OR 97116
503-359-4010
www.olsonsbicycles.com
Whatever you need, Mike will fix you up.

ACCOMMODATIONS

<u>PRICE KEY</u>
   * = < $100
   ** = $100-175
   *** = $200-300
   **** = >$300

<u>Bed and Breakfast</u>

Le Puy Inn ***/****
20300 NE Highway 240
Newberg, OR 97132
503-554-9528
www.lepuy-inn.com

Hosts (owners): Lea and Andy Duffy

This eight guest room bed & breakfast has beautifully manicured grounds with a bubbling stone and water sculpture in its courtyard entrance. It provides a panoramic view north and west of the valley. Leah can point out individual wineries from the large and comfortably appointed Great Room.

Le Puy offers a bike package for an addition $90. This includes a hybrid bicycle, a sack lunch, and your choices of maps to destinations close by. Leah has many recommendations for wineries to visit and will set up reservations at wineries not open to the public (given a two week notice).

Lodge/Hotel

Grand Lodge McMenamins */**/***
3505 Pacific Ave, Forest Grove, OR 97116
877-992-9533 or 503-992-9533
www.mcmenamin.com/55-grand-lodge

Another McMenamins renovation, the Grand Lodge, built in 1922, was once a Masonic and Eastern Star home. The walls feature colorful artwork and historical photographs. There are 77 European-style guest rooms, some with private baths, others with a common bath down the hall. There are restaurants and bars, live music, movies – something for everyone.

Resort

The Allison Inn ***/****
2525 Allison Lane
Newberg, OR 97132
877-294-2525 or 503-294-2525
www.theallison.com/inn

Deluxe all the way. If you want to be pampered, this is your place. There are spa and salon services. The restaurant features Northwest cuisine and local wines. Explore the seasonal packages they offer. The resort has a locked storage for your bike, if you wish, or you might elect to have a first floor room with patio for your bike.

Places to Stay in the Gorge

If you wish to stay east of Portland in the Columbia River Gorge, there are a variety of places in Hood River worth checking out. However, remember to book ahead. It seems everyone is looking for a place to stay in Hood River, with peak seasons being summer and winter.

Villa Columbia B&B **
902 Oak Street
Hood River, OR 97031
541-386-6670
www.villacolumbia.com

Host (owners): VJ and Boba

Five rooms in a turn-of-the-century mission-style home, complete with original dark wood paneling, deep, comfortable sofas, and lots of windows to gaze down to the river. There is plenty of room for 14 people to sit down to eat. There is an inside area to store bikes (and wind-surfing gear). There is also off-street parking. Boba, your hostess, is happy to give you suggestions for your day if you ask.

Hood River Hotel **/***
102 Oak Street
Hood River, OR 97031
541-386-1900
www.hoodriverhotel.com

Hood River Hotel, in the heart of downtown, is a landmark building, built in 1911. It retains much of the original charm but with modern conveniences. There are 41 guest rooms. Some are suites, some have kitchenettes. If it's important that your bike stay with you, let them know. Bikes can be taken to some of the rooms. If you choose, you need not look for a place to eat in the morning. The dining room is open for breakfast and lunch, and all day on Sunday. Parking passes are issued for $5/day.

For other B&Bs check out www.oregonwineinns.com and www.bedandbreakfast.com/hood-river-oregon

SHIPPING WINE

Newberg Mail Room

1102 N. Springbrook Road

Newberg OR 97132

503-538-5555

www.newbergmailroom.com

Acknowledgments

Thanks to Andie Long for believing these rides were worth publishing, for exploring some of the wineries with me, for her photography skills, and for her editing prowess.

Thanks to Scott Atwood at SmartLocalMedia.com who spent endless hours researching the self-publishing world, scouting out various vendors to help, teaching me new tech skills, and ultimately for getting this book published in its various forms.

Thanks to all the people along the way, the tasting room associates, the owners of the bed and breakfasts, inns and other places for overnighting. Thanks to the many bicycle shops I frequented for information. A special thanks to Veloce Bicycle for setting me up with a bike that could cheerfully climb the gravel roads that I explored. Thanks to Ride with GPS for their permission to use their maps, and all the other support their website provides. Thanks to all of those who read the manuscript and pointed out ways to make the book better.

ABOUT THE AUTHOR

My first foray into bicycle riding was an almost seven month adventure in 1975, when I set out to "do Europe" on $5 dollars a day. It was during this time that I inadvertently developed a passion for wine. In all the countries I visited wine was, of course, not a luxury, but very much part of the meal. Back in the U.S. I found the wine industry just developing and its quality was spotty. Lucky for me I moved to the Willamette Valley in 1979, just as many of the pioneers of Pinot Noir were beginning to sell wine commercially.

For the next decade bicycling and fine wine took a back seat to my career and child rearing. By the early 1990's however, I picked up bicycling again. I joined several bicycle clubs and began logging hundreds of miles. I completed Seattle-to-Portland (STP) several times, as well as Cycle Oregon, Bike Vermont, Oregon Bike and numerous other "century" rides in the Willamette Valley. Additionally, I took on multi-week bicycle tours in Italy and France. The Willamette Valley has been my training ground for long-distance riding, and as I gained seniority in the bicycle clubs, I began mapping-out and leading a variety of rides for the group.

In 2007 I enrolled at Oregon's Chemeketa Community College in the vineyard management and wine-making program. Here I hoped to transform my passion for wine into an encore career. By 2012 I decided to set myself a goal that would allow me to combine both my passions: bicycling and wine. I would write a bicycle wine touring book!

Many wine makers in the Willamette Valley and most notable Yamhill County have begun to emphasize sustainability both in their grape-growing and their wine production. I knew I wanted to emphasize these wineries in particular. I had visited and loved some of them, but there were many I had yet to discover.

I decided for the book I would map out 10 rides that included visits to sustainable, organic, and biodynamic wineries. But how many wineries to include on each ride? And how many miles should each ride cover? Where would people from out of town stay? And where could they rent bikes, or have them shipped from home?

As I dove into the research, I began to uncover interesting tidbits on the towns the rides passed through. Who knew that the town of Yamhill had the first electric lights outside of Portland? Or, that the Pretty Good Grocery in Gaston makes gourmet sandwiches on baguettes?

Suffice it to say, it's been quite a journey and I hope that the rides in this book kindle in others the same kind of passion I feel for great wine and great winemaking.

Made in United States
North Haven, CT
06 June 2022